SO-AWM-274

The Insiders Guide To Air Courier Bargains

How to travel world-wide
for next to nothing

by
Kelly Monaghan

The Insiders Guide
To Air Courier Bargains
✈ ✈ ✈
How To Travel World-Wide
For Next To Nothing

Published by:
Inwood Training Publications
Post Office Box 438
New York, NY 10034, USA

All rights reserved. No part of this book may be reproduced or transmitted in any form or by any means, electronic or mechanical, including photocopying, recording or by any information storage and retrieval system without the express written permission of the author, except for the inclusion of brief quotations in a review.

Copyright © 1992 by Kelly Monaghan
Second Edition
First Printing, January, 1992
Printed in the United States of America
Cover design: Derek McCabe

Library of Congress Catalog Card Number: 91-075580

ISBN: 0-9627892-6-7

ACKNOWLEDGMENTS

I would like to extend my sincere thanks to Roger Johansen, who helped out with the London research, my loving son Niall, and especially to Sally Scanlon, whose keen editorial eye and unfailing encouragement sustained me throughout the creative process.

— KM

TABLE OF CONTENTS

PLEASE NOTE

Although the author and the publisher have made every effort to insure the completeness and accuracy of this guide, we assume no responsibility for omissions, inaccuracies, errors, or inconsistencies that may appear. All slights of people or organizations are unintentional.

It must be understood that the listings in this guide in no way constitute an endorsement or guarantee on the part of the author or publisher. All readers who deal with the courier companies listed herein do so at their own risk.

Flying as a freelance courier involves a contractual relationship between the courier and the courier company. This book is sold with the understanding that neither the author nor the publisher are engaged in rendering legal or other professional advice. If legal or other expert assistance is required, the reader should consult with a competent professional.

The author and Inwood Training Publications shall have neither liability nor responsibility to any person or entity with respect to any loss or damage caused, or alleged to be caused, directly or indirectly, by the information contained herein.

Lessons Learned

A bout the time the first edition of *The Insiders Guide To Air Courier Bargains* was hitting the bookstores, the civilized world went charging into Kuwait and the world of travel went into a tailspin. I learned a very important lesson in the process: Times of trouble are terrific times to travel.

Travel to Europe from the United States and England was way off due to the fear of terrorism. The result was a slew of bargains for fearless travelers. Airlines, eager to recoup lost business, lowered fares; hotels, desperate to fill empty rooms, offered substantial discounts. But if there were savings for everyone, there were super-bargains for couriers. During this period, I noted $99 round trip courier fares from New York to Geneva, Copenhagen, Amsterdam and Madrid — even to London and Paris where discounts of any sort tend to be rare.

And how many of these couriers fell prey to terrorists? None. Zero. Naught. Zilch.

I noticed a similar phenomenon when Mount Pinatubo erupted in the Philippines. One courier company started allowing couriers on its Manila run to take two pieces of checked baggage (they paid the excess baggage fees for their own cargo). The reason: fewer people wanted to visit the Philippines while it was raining ash. The fact that Manila was little affected didn't seem to matter.

There is another lesson I learned—or more accurately *re*learned — since the first edition was published: The courier business is constantly changing.

U.S. domestic flights are now seemingly a thing of the past. Athens, Oslo, and Dublin seem to have dropped off the map as courier destinations in the wake of problems created by the Gulf War and economic changes in the courier business itself.

Companies are constantly expanding, contracting, and redefining themselves. One company that flew to Seoul, Korea, and Sydney, Australia, a year ago, now flies only to Manila. Others have stopped offering flights from some cities they used to serve. Several other courier companies have disappeared without a trace into the black hole of disconnected telephones and "no forwarding address."

On the other hand, new sources of courier bookings have come into being. Some companies have opened branches in new cities, to serve new markets. A major new booking agency has opened in New York. A new source of flights to Seoul has cropped up in Los Angeles. The second edition provides all the details.

So let me say it here first and then repeat it throughout the book: "Things change." As you call around to enquire about flights you may find—in fact, probably will find—that phone numbers and addresses have changed, fares have changed, routes have changed, and on and on. You may even find that some companies no longer exist.

Nonetheless, you will find that many opportunities remain and many great bargains are still to be had. Good luck and happy contrails to you.

10

Chapter One

Introduction

I pulled up my collar and smiled. I was on my way to London. In coach, yes, but certainly not as a mere tourist. I was an air courier!

Call me a romantic, but the very words — *air courier* — filled me with anticipation. As I strode purposefully into the terminal, I could hear Peter Lorre whispering to me from *Casablanca*. "Letters of transit. Signed by General DeGaulle himself. Cannot be rescinded."

I slid into a phone booth. Following instructions to the letter, I dialed a number and asked for Vince. No last name. Just Vince. We couriers are a cagey bunch.

"I'll send someone right over," Vince assured me. "Name's Danny. Meet him at the cashier's desk opposite gate one. What are you wearing so I can tell him?"

I gave Vince the lowdown. Trench coat. (I told you I was a romantic.) White shirt. Blue tie. I began to regret I hadn't thought to wear a red carnation.

I lounged against the wall by the cashier's desk and surveyed the crowd. How many, I wondered, were on a secret mission like me? And what would Danny be like? A rotund Sidney Greenstreet or a suave Paul Henreid?

"Mr. Monaghan?" Another in a long line of illusions was shattered. Danny was a scrawny, unassuming teenager, hardly a character out of a Bogart film.

Danny handed me my ticket and got me checked in. He gave me a large white plastic pouch emblazoned with the logo of a courier company. My letters of transit, I assumed.

"It's empty," I observed.

"Yeah. Hold it up when you come out of customs in London so they'll be able to identify you," Danny explained.

"What am I transporting?" I dared to ask.

"Tell you the truth, I don't know."

I settled into my seat in coach and looked around. Now that my trench coat was stowed in the overhead I looked like just another (sigh) tourist. "At least I'm on the aisle," I thought and closed my eyes.

I arrived in London wondering if I would be humiliated in customs as "my" checked luggage yielded up some guilty secret while drug-sniffing dogs yapped in pleasure. Instead I was waved through without so much as a glance.

I soon made contact with London's version of Danny. He addressed me in fluent Cockney and escorted me to a small warehouse-like building ringed with courier vans. After a short wait, I was informed that everything was in order and I was free to go. As I walked toward the tube station for my trip into London, I felt let down. This wasn't the last reel of *Casablanca*. No rolling fog on the tarmac. No Ingrid Bergman. No romance.

The truth was simply that flying as an air courier was a cut and dried business proposition that got me to London on short notice for a mere fraction of what it would have cost otherwise. And that, I decided, was good enough for me.

S ince that first flight to London, I have become an avid courier traveler. I have even discovered an element of "romance" in the process. It's not so much in the actual travel — which is not much different from the experience of the "tourists" sitting next to you. The real payoff, I have learned, is in the reaction of my friends.

"You did what?" they asked incredulously.

"I went trout fishing in Venezuela for a week," I replied casually. "In the high lakes, they have some real nice ten-pounders."

At first, I'd explain myself by adding, "Of course, it was dirt cheap. I went as an air courier. Only cost me $175." That, naturally, led to a cascade of questions.

"Air courier? $175? *Round-trip?* How did you manage that? Tell me about it. What were you doing, transporting drugs? Really? How can *I* do that?"

Eventually, I learned to keep my mouth shut. Partly, I admit, it was to avoid answering all the questions. But just between you and me, I enjoy letting people think that the $250 fare to London, the $50 to Antigua, the $150 to Stockholm — all round-trips — had cost much, *much* more.

I used to think that air courier travel was just for special people — like me! — but as I learned the ropes and met more and more of my fellow couriers, I learned that there are no hard and fast rules about who is traveling as a courier. The old saying, "it takes all kinds to make a world" is just as true about the air courier business.

Are *you* cut out to be an air courier? You might be if you are ...

• **A student.** Or anyone else with time on their hands and not a lot of money. Students and other young people have a natural desire to see the world and the flexible schedules that let them take advantage of the opportunities offered by air courier travel. Graduate students can use courier flights to do on-the-spot research that might be impossible at full fare.

• **A senior citizen or retiree.** The 'golden years' need not mean just a rocking chair on a quiet porch. Senior citizens are much sought after by courier companies. Their reputation for promptness and reliability makes them especially desirable. One gentleman on the West coast has seen much of the Orient thanks to low-cost courier fares. Why not stretch those retirement dollars and indulge your taste for world travel?

• **A freelancer.** If you work on a freelance basis, I don't have to tell you how difficult it is to plan vacations. Just when you hope to get away, a big project comes in. The air courier option actually works in the favor of the freelancer.

Here's a perfect way to reward yourself when a block of time opens up in your schedule. And there's another bonus: The shorter the notice, the cheaper the fare. You can finish a project one day and fly out the next using the strategies revealed in *The Insiders Guide.*

• **A teacher.** Many teachers looked forward to tax-deductible travel during the summer. That was before "tax simplification."

But while the IRS has curtailed travel deductions for teachers, air courier fares are still low, low, low. If the new tax rules made you think you couldn't afford to travel abroad to hone your teaching skills, think again.

• **An entrepreneur.** Like the freelancer, the entrepreneur cannot plan vacations months in advance. But entrepreneurs often want to explore overseas markets and keep costs down.

Many importers find air courier travel a dollar-saving strategy for exploring new opportunities or keeping in close touch with existing suppliers. If you have a product line that can be exported, courier travel can provide a low-cost way of exploring new markets and visiting potential buyers.

• **An enthusiast.** Are you a bicyclist who's dreamed of seeing the Tour de France? An opera buff who wants to visit La Scala? An arm-chair archaeologist who will never see Machu Picchu? Sometimes the only thing that stands in the way of realizing a long-cherished dream is the high cost of air travel. Being an air courier eliminates that obstacle. Feel free to dream when you travel as an air courier.

• **Ready for a change.** Air courier bargains are designed for the solo traveler. Are you ready for a change of pace? Is it high time you got away, by yourself, to relax or think things over? A week alone on a foreign beach can work wonders!

• **A smart shopper.** Even if you don't need to pinch pennies, air courier travel can expand your travel horizons. After all, the $500 (or more!) you save on airfare can pay for that luxury hotel you've always wanted to stay in but thought you could never afford! Or the same amount of money you budgeted for a weekend getaway close to home could take you to Mexico for a week!

• **Adventurous.** Let's face it, "beating the system" is fun! Picking up the phone and saying, "I'm available. What's the next flight out?" can bring the kind of thrills that well-planned vacations never offer.

It really *is* possible to indulge your taste for world travel and pay one-half, one-third, even one-tenth the cost of regular coach fares. Sometimes it is even possible to fly for the next best thing to "free."

This book tells you how.

Chapter Two

The Air Courier Business

C ouriers, of one sort or another, have a long and proud history. The earliest use of the word in English, cited in the *Oxford English Dictionary*, occurs in Wyclif's *Chronicles* of 1382 — "Curours wenten with letters."

Not much has changed in the last 600 years. Today, couriers still "go with letters." But today the distances couriers cover are truly global, the demand for expedited delivery vastly increased, and the medieval runner has been replaced by the modern air courier, traveling coach on jet airplanes.

Historically, couriers were used for military and diplomatic communications. In 1579, it was recorded that the Pope was making use of "dayly curriers and postes." In the seventeenth century, every military command had its "courier at arms." Alexander Hamilton and the Duke of Wellington both mention their use of couriers.

Of course, the diplomatic and commercial interests of great nations often coincided and diplomats and diplomatic couriers, with the immunity from search they enjoyed, became conduits for merchants with connections in high places. "Eventually," says Lawrence Burtchaell, Executive Director of the Air Courier

Conference of America (ACCA), an industry group, "the diplomatic courier became a commercial courier carrying shipments for clients in pouches as his own baggage." The advent of the airplane just added a new wrinkle to an already well-established business practice. Indeed, carrying letters and documents was one of the first commercial uses to which the new-fangled flying machine was put. Today, of course, this specialized form of expedited delivery is a major industry.

"Air couriers, as we understand the term today, began in the sixties," explains Burtchaell. "When we began, 99% of what we carried was documents. Ninety percent of the courier companies would not handle high value stuff because it was too dangerous — they had couriers who actually ended up in the river. So most of them refused to carry things like gold and jewelry. What they were taking were documents that had to move very rapidly. It was all based on time-sensitive material. The postal services were very bad, and they still are for that matter."

It remains the same today. High-value articles are handled by specialists like Brinks Air Courier which uses highly-trained couriers and has developed special procedures to insure the safe arrival of valuable cargo. Most air courier shipments are decidedly mundane. Time-sensitive materials, of little value to anyone other than the sender and receiver, are placed aboard regularly scheduled commercial airliners as passenger's baggage. They are accompanied on the flight by an individual — usually referred to in the industry as an "on-board courier" or simply "OBC" — who carries the paperwork for the shipment.

But why are on-board couriers needed at all? Can't things be sent air freight without needing someone to accompany the shipment? Of course they can, but there are two factors which have combined to create a niche for the on-board courier in the air freight business.

18

The first is the airlines themselves. "There are only two ways you can get your material on an aircraft," explains Martin Mosley, Vice President of Line Haul at TNT Express Worldwide. "With a passenger as excess baggage or as general cargo.

"With general cargo, you normally have a lock-out time of four or five hours prior to plane departure," he continues. That is the latest the airline will accept cargo for a particular flight. "Your material has to be manifested by the airline and consolidated with other shipments in those big silver containers you see being trundled around the airport.

"As a passenger, you can arrive less than sixty minutes before departure and, depending on the security of the airport you're at, get your material on the plane."

The differences continue at the other end. "When the plane lands, passengers' baggage comes off first," Mosley notes. "Twenty or thirty minutes later, your baggage is whizzing around the carousel for you to pick it up.

"The containers come off second. Then they have to be towed to a cargo facility, where they are opened, broken down, and segregated on shelves so that when people come with their airbills to collect their material and clear it, the material will be available for them to do that.

"That normally takes — at an absolute minimum — three or four hours. And, more realistically, at airports like Heathrow [in London], with the volumes they're dealing with, twelve hours is the norm."

The result, Mosley concludes, is being able to offer TNT's customers two and a half or three day service instead of overnight delivery. And that's simply not good enough.

The other major factor in creating a need for on-board couriers is what John Wilson of Speedbird Courier refers to as "that dinosaur, the customs official." Not only does cargo have to get off the plane, it has to be cleared through customs.

No matter how complex or archaic a country's customs regulations are — and according to Burtchaell some of them are truly bizarre — a basic distinction is made between passengers' baggage and regular air cargo.

Once again, the most important factor is time. "Courier companies are in the business of express delivery," explains Courier Travel Services in London. "Much of the courier material is made up of documents, mail, computer software and so on, that are urgently required elsewhere in the world. Couriers are required so that the material can be moved as check-in passenger baggage, which if otherwise went as air cargo can take up to three days to clear."

International packages sent via regular air freight can sit in bonded airport warehouses for days before they clear customs I am told. This also increases the likelihood of pilferage or loss. The baggage of a passenger on a regularly scheduled flight, on the other hand, goes through customs as soon as the plane lands. Many companies are happy to pay the additional charges to use an on-board courier service and make sure their valuable papers and packages arrive as quickly and safely as possible, on a scheduled flight.

M any companies offer overnight, world-wide shipment, and many companies list themselves in the Yellow Pages under "Air Courier Services." They range in size from global giants like Federal Express to local mom-and-pop operations.

The major players in the industry, like Federal Express and DHL, are vertically integrated. That is, *their* employee picks up your package at your office, transports it in *their* van to the airport, and puts its aboard *their* plane. When the plane lands at its foreign destination, *their* employees unload it, *their* representatives clear the package through customs, place it in one of *their* vans, and one of *their* employees hand-delivers it to the person to whom you have sent it. These companies seldom, if ever, have a need for on-board couriers — at least to major foreign destinations.

Very few of the other companies, regardless of their size, actually handle the nitty-gritty details of getting an overnight shipment onto a plane. Instead, they turn over the overseas packages they receive to someone else and take a cut of the fee for finding the customer.

Many companies that bill themselves as "air courier" firms actually turn over their expedited shipments to someone like Federal Express, which charges them wholesale rates for their shipments. Others will turn to an air freight "wholesaler" like Halbart in New York or Speedbird in London. Very few companies see the shipment through the air courier process themselves.

[By the way, full details on Halbart, Speedbird, and other courier companies mentioned in the text will be found in the "International Air Courier Directory" in Part II of *The Insiders Guide*.]

An air courier wholesaler deals strictly with the mechanics of expedited air shipments; their customers are other shippers and not the general public. They have specialized in the detailed business of finding the couriers, negotiating wholesale tariffs with the airlines based on volume, booking the flights to get the packages overseas, and coordinating the whole operation. Many of their employees are bonded and carry special identification that allows them "behind the scenes" access. Because of their close contact with airline and customs personnel, these companies can offer freight forwarders a valuable service by speeding shipments into and out of the airports they serve.

A typical shipment sent out by a wholesaler will contain pouches from several different courier companies. This is known as co-loading. When the shipment arrives at its destination, each pouch will be picked up by a representative authorized to receive it. Larger companies, like Airborne, may have their own representatives at either end. Smaller companies may have reciprocal arrangements; in other words, the shipment from Joe's Courier Company in New York will be picked up by Fred's Courier Company in London, and vice versa.

Another category of air courier is the "retailer." Retailers go into the market to solicit business and then handle the courier shipments themselves. World Courier in New York is an example of this type of operation. Typically, retailers deal with larger business customers who ship in volume and who prefer the special attention and extra level of reassurance a retailer can provide. They are not interested in the onesy-twosy type of business; Federal Express handles that. Retailers may also co-load pouches from other companies with their own shipments.

As you can see, while there are many "air couriers" there are relatively few companies that actually deal with on-board couriers. A situation which can be problematical for the budget traveler, as we shall see.

C ourier companies make their money on the difference between what they charge their customers to ship something overseas and their actual cost of shipping it. It works out something like this: A typical charge for the trans-Atlantic shipment of a one pound "letter" is $25. It costs the courier company approximately $1 dollar in freight charges by the airline to send that letter across the ocean, based on their putting 16,000 pounds of freight on a specific flight each week. Pickup and delivery costs at either end add another $10. So far, the courier company is left with $14 in gross profit.

Out of that profit comes the related costs of shipping the letter — the envelope it's sent in, the airbill, manifesting, bagging, payroll, trucking, the on-board courier's ticket, and miscellaneous overhead — which costs approximately $5 or $6 per letter.

Added to this is corporate overhead — executive staff, middle management, marketing, sales, customer service, and so forth — which accounts for an additional $3 or $4 per letter.

That means that after all expenses, $4 to $6 is left over as pre-tax profit. This may have to be shared among several parties, with the company that picks the letter up, the wholesaler who ships it, and the company that delivers it on the other end each taking their share.

Other customer service or collection problems may eat into this profit. "It costs $15 just to raise and invoice and collect a debt," claims one courier company insider. "By the time we've finished costing out an individual express letter, we may have lost $20 on the movement. And the only way we can bring that back into profit is volume."

The volume can be impressive. I once arrived in New York as a courier accompanying 87 pouches, and one pouch can contain 70 or 100 pounds of cargo. And that was on one flight. World-wide, there are scores of courier flights every day. On the London-New

York axis alone there are something like 160 rotations each week. By any measure, air couriers are big business.

Obviously, courier companies have good reasons to want their customers to believe that they are operating under the thinnest possible margins in providing them with this valuable service. But I tend to agree with the assessment of ACCA's Burtchaell.

"It's a very lucrative business," he says.

A s we noted earlier, the need for on-board couriers arises from a need for expedited delivery, on the one hand, and the hidebound attitudes of the airlines and customs on the other. "How can we ship it as passengers' baggage without a passenger?" asks the airline. "How can I clear it as passengers' baggage without a passenger?" asks the customs agent.

The air freight company sighs and looks around for a passenger. And every year they have to come up with thousands of them. Where do they all come from?

Some are full-time employees of the courier companies. In the case of a specialist company like Brinks, there's no other way to do it. You can't entrust a million dollars in diamonds to just anyone. Brinks' couriers, however, have other duties and don't just spend their working lives on planes.

Some companies, that need on-boards only infrequently, will use their own people. In these cases, courier travel can be a perk (or a hidden liability!) of employment. And some companies actually employ full-time couriers whose job it is to fly from Point A to Point B and back again in the shortest possible period of time.

If you've set yourself the goal of reading every one of the World's Great Books, this might be a job worth having. Otherwise, I find it hard to imagine a duller job.

For most companies involved in the courier business, having full-time couriers on their payroll is not a viable option. Instead, they look outside. Many, if not most, on-board couriers are "casual couriers," part-timers like me — or you! A "casual courier," as defined by IBC-Pacific in their courier instructions, is simply "a person who accompanies time-sensitive business cargo that is checked on board an aircraft as excess baggage."

It's a marriage of convenience. The courier company needs someone to sit in the seat and carry out the minimal duties of carrying the paperwork. Thousands of budget-conscious travelers, on the other hand, are looking for a cheap way to get overseas.

In the distant past (15 years or so), you could actually get paid to be a casual courier. "We used to *employ* people," says TNT's Mosley with a hint of amazement in his voice. "They used to fly Club and we'd pay for their hotels and everything!"

Then the courier companies discovered that there were people who were more than happy to give up their checked luggage allotment for a free ticket. Then some clever person (may he burn in fires eternal!) figured out that they could charge couriers a fee and still get takers.

"We discovered we could do it," says one courier company official matter-of-factly. "The key to any business is to charge what the traffic will bear."

So today the courier company has an additional interest in seeking outside, freelance couriers — the courier can offset some of the expense of the ticket.

I am fascinated by the connotations the word "courier" has taken on in the popular imagination. For some, it conjures up visions of someone with a trench coat buttoned up to here with a leather briefcase handcuffed to their wrist. Others, who have obviously watched one episode too many of *Miami Vice*, cannot hear the word "courier" without thinking "drugs."

Once you begin traveling as an air courier, I can virtually guarantee that your friends will start asking whether or not you're transporting something at least mildly suspect — especially if you tell them how little you paid for your ticket.

The fact of the matter is that the air courier business is just as mundane as any other. It goes on day in, day out, year after year. It has well-established, cut-and-dried procedures that are carried out to the letter, with a high priority placed on safety and legality.

Would-be couriers can take comfort in the knowledge that the airlines require the courier companies to invest in extremely expensive x-ray machines to screen every pouch that's put aboard their planes. Customs, for its part, knows that smugglers are unlikely to send contraband through a channel in which the sender and recipient are so well identified.

"We have found contraband in these shipments," says U.S. Customs official Bob Fischler, "but percentage-wise it's infinitesimal. And in any seizure we made, it was obvious to us that the on-board courier had nothing to do with it." In fact, at New York's

JFK and at London's Heathrow airports, because of the sheer volume of courier shipments, all courier pouches go to a central location for clearance. The courier has usually been dismissed before customs physically inspects the shipments.

For as long as I've been traveling as a courier, people have been predicting the imminent demise of the courier business — at least from the standpoint of the freelance on-board courier.

"The fax machine will put an end to the need for couriers," was one theory. Yet the fax seems to have had little impact. For one thing, objects cannot be faxed. Many businesses are reluctant to fax signed contracts, except for informational purposes. And once a document reaches a certain length, it's cheaper to send it by courier than to fax it. Fax technology may, in fact, have increased awareness in the business community of the importance of getting things back and forth in a timely fashion and actually helped the courier business.

A more likely reason for courier flights to dry up is simple economics and the changing patterns of business. For any given courier run there will be a tonnage figure at which the route becomes profitable. In other words, if you can ship "x" number of tons of expedited cargo to Dublin you will make money. Once the tonnage slips below that figure, the route will cease to become worthwhile and cargo will be shipped by another, less timely, method. "If they don't have enough weight — and it simply comes down to literal weight — then they can't afford to [use a courier]," says Julie Weinberg of Now Voyager in New York. "They have to send it without purchasing an actual plane ticket."

27

That's what has happened in the past year or so not only to Dublin but to Athens and Oslo as well. The air courier companies in New York found there was not enough demand to justify keeping the service open. (Athens is still a courier run from London.)

But while some routes close down, others open up. Geneva is a new destination from New York and I hear predictions that we will soon see service to Moscow and the newly emerging countries of the eastern Bloc. Sources in London confidently predict that there will soon be flights from there to South America.

Of greater impact to the would-be courier are efforts to circumvent the air freight stumbling blocks that gave rise to the need for couriers in the first place. Some airlines have made a pitch for courier business by instituting special categories of air freight which will receive expedited handling. Australian customs, for one, has recognized the special realities of international business and begun providing expedited clearance; one result is that courier flights to Australia have declined.

While some courier runs may now be closed to the freelance on-board courier, there are still thousands of flights each year which need ordinary people like you and me to serve as couriers.

Chapter Three

Getting Started

M any people who are interested in traveling internationally as air couriers begin by picking up the trusty Yellow Pages and looking under the "Air Courier Services" listing. It sounds logical, but they are making a fundamental mistake.

The companies that have themselves listed under the "Air Courier Services" heading in the Yellow Pages are not looking for people who want to travel cheap. Instead, they are looking for people or, more likely, companies that want to ship time-sensitive papers, packages, or commodities overseas.

Most of these companies are not true air couriers at all but what are known in the industry as "forwarders." They get the business and then "contract it out" to other companies that handle the actual air courier part of the transaction.

Moreover, these companies tend to be very poor sources of information about flying as a courier. For one thing, the people answering the phone may have absolutely no idea what happens to the packages they accept for shipment. For another, these companies have a vested interest in obscuring their mode of operation.

It all has to do with image. A recent television commercial for DHL offers a perfect illustration of what the shippers in the industry want you to think of them: A DHL van is seen speeding through the air, passing an airliner in flight. Part of the message is speed. But DHL is also pushing the idea that, once you place your valuable package in their van, it stays there until it is delivered on the other side of the ocean. Regardless of how they actually operate, all freight companies want to convey this idea of total door-to-door service.

That's why when you ask about being a courier they will say things like, "We use our own people," or "We have special arrangements with the airlines," or "We don't reveal that information." Nor are they likely to refer you elsewhere — other companies are, after all, their competition.

After calling dozens of companies, only to be told that they don't use freelance couriers, never have, never will, and don't know anyone who does, you will start to think that these rumors you've heard about super low-cost fares are a fantasy — either that, or someone's lying to you. Neither is true. Just remember that most of the companies listed in the Yellow Pages want to hear from people willing to pay a premium fee to ship important packages and not people who want to pay very little to ship themselves.

The "International Air Courier Directory" in Part II of *The Insiders Guide* will save you hours of fruitless phoning to companies that don't want to hear from you and may be rude when you reach them. Some of the contacts listed in the directory aren't even listed in the phone book.

The first thing the would-be courier needs is a passport. If you don't already have a passport, don't think you can wait until you have booked a flight to apply for one. Most courier companies will ask you to prove that you have a passport before they'll give you a ticket. Some require you to provide them with a photocopy. I keep on hand several photocopies of the two pages of my passport that have my photo and personal information. That way I can present a photocopy or send one through the mail to assure the courier company that I have a valid passport. It's not a bad idea to have a photocopy in any case. If your passport is ever lost or stolen, having a photocopy can speed up the process of getting it replaced.

Generally speaking, nationality is no bar to courier travel, just so long as your papers are in order. In other words, you do not have to be an American citizen to fly as an air courier through an American air courier company, although some have different requirements for those holding non-U.S. passports. (See the "International Air Courier Directory" for details.) I have also been assured by courier companies in Canada and the United Kingdom that Americans can take advantage of their courier flights.

If you will be traveling to a country that requires a visa, you must make your own arrangements and prove to the courier company that you have the required documentation. Often, the courier company will alert you that a visa is required but the responsibility is yours, so it's wise to double check. It is a simple matter to check on visa requirements by calling the embassy or consulate of the country involved.

For American citizens, I would recommend the State Department publication, *Foreign Visa Requirements*, which lists entry requirements and application instructions for most countries. It is available for 50 cents from the Consumer Information Center,

Dept. 438T, Pueblo, CO, 81009. Those who are carrying other than American passports must do their own research as to what the visa requirements are; you cannot expect the courier company to do it for you or even to provide you with information.

Passport in hand, you are ready to take your first courier trip. But to where? It helps to have a general awareness of where you can fly as a courier.

As I noted earlier, the existence of a courier run between two cities is a function of demand, which in turn results from business patterns. If there is sufficient commerce between two cities or countries to make courier service economically viable, then it is more than likely that a courier company will attempt to tap that market.

From the United States, you can reach every continent except Africa as a courier. Far and away the most available destination is London, with flights from New York, Miami, Houston, San Francisco, and Los Angeles. Otherwise, you will most likely find certain destinations available only from certain gateways: Europe from New York, South America from Miami, and the Orient from Vancouver, San Francisco, and Los Angeles.

From London, there is a different pattern, reflecting different patterns of commerce. A great many cities in the United States are available from London, while relatively few destinations on the European continent are offered. Because of the short distances involved, most courier flights to the continent from London are handled by employees who go and come on the same day. Flights to Africa, however, where England maintains close commercial ties to its former colonies, are available. There are no flights to South America at present, as there were in the past, although that may change I am told.

Other factors may also influence the availability of courier flights. For example, no one (to my knowledge) is offering seats for freelance couriers to the Indian subcontinent. The reason, I am told, is that customs regulations in that part of the world are so strict that courier companies are forced to use professional, bonded couriers on these runs. Recent changes in Australian customs policies, making it easier to send expedited air cargo without an on-board courier have resulted in the decline (but not the disappearance) of courier slots to destinations like Sydney.

As you may have guessed by now, courier travel is an international phenomenon. Clearing customs, obviously, is not a consideration when you are shipping parcels from New York to Los Angeles. Nonetheless, it was not too long ago that courier slots were available between New York and LA, as well as between LA and Miami. Here's how it worked:

A niche in the market was created by the perceived unreliability of "over-the-counter" air freight offered by the airlines, on the one hand, and the relatively low cost of a passenger's ticket, on the other. A few entrepreneurial companies, such as Now Courier of Los Angeles, saw an opportunity to say to businesses which shipped in volume, "Look, send your stuff with us. We'll guarantee faster delivery than you're currently getting from the airlines and it will cost you less to boot." The entrepreneur would then purchase a ticket and send the freight as excess passenger's baggage. An additional factor made this arrangement viable: the courier company could make these courier seats available to employees of its customer firms at no cost! It was a win-win solution all around.

According to Julie Weinberg of Now Voyager, which used to book these flights, economic realities closed the market niche. The airlines improved the reliability of their air freight and made the cost more competitive while the cost of a passenger's ticket rose. The courier runs ceased to be viable and the service ended.

"If market conditions change, we may see these flights becoming available again," notes Weinberg. You may want to check in with Now Voyager's recorded information from time to time. (See the "International Air Courier Directory" in Part II for details.)

Now you must decide where you want to go and when you want to go there. Making this decision is not quite so obvious as it may seem. There are three main ways to plan your air courier travel and the one you choose will determine your strategy in locating and booking a flight.

You can settle on a destination and *approximate* dates on which you would like to leave and return. Most of the companies listed in this guide will be most comfortable in dealing with you if you have a fairly firm idea of where and about when you want to go.

Another approach is to choose a destination and then fly there when a flight becomes available. That could be immediately or three months from now. Most companies don't book flights more than three months in advance, although some have schedules stretching almost six months into the future. You may be forced into this choice with certain high-demand, low-availability destinations such as Tel Aviv. You will have to monitor flight availability with the few companies that fly there and jump on the flight that best meets your schedule.

Finally, you can choose a date or dates on which you will be available to travel and pick from the destinations available at the time. The sooner you book, the wider selection you will have. The longer you wait, the more likely you will be to find a bargain fare.

Once you have decided on which strategy will work best for you, your next step is to get in touch with a courier contact that offers flights to the destination or on the dates of your choice. You can either deal directly with a courier company or use one of the various booking agencies that serve as middlemen in the courier industry.

I would recommend that, all things being equal, beginners use the booking agents, especially in New York. There are several reasons for this:

- The convenience of one-stop shopping. Many booking agents offer more destinations than any one of the individual courier companies they represent.

- The booking agents are used to dealing with beginners. Part of what they get paid for is patiently explaining what courier travel is all about and helping you through the process.

- Getting information can be easier. The booking agent doesn't make money unless you book a flight; so, in theory at least, he or she has a certain incentive to give you as much information as you need to make a decision and book a flight. The harried air courier operator, on the other hand, may know that the demand for seats is high enough to ensure that he'll get the couriers he needs, even if he doesn't take time out of his busy day to answer your questions.

- Sometimes it's the only way. In some instances, the courier company designates an agency as its sole representative. In other situations, you may not know which company to call directly for a flight to a city you want. The booking agents make it their business to monitor the industry and locate new opportunities for their customers.

- Additional services that are not available from the courier companies. For example, Courier Travel Service in New York or Shades International Travel in England can book you onto a flight that will get you to your courier flight. Also, the booking agencies that used to specialize exclusively in courier flights are branching out into other bargain travel niches, offering charter flights and special fares from the airlines.

The only real negative of dealing with a booking agent is the fee that some of them charge. In the case of Now Voyager, in New York, the fee is large enough ($50 annually) to make you think twice. If you fly only once a year to a $199 destination, you have instantly increased the effective cost of your flight by 25 percent! Of course, the more you fly, the less of an issue the registration fee becomes. Also the "year" is determined by when you book a flight not when you actually fly. So you can book a flight the day before your membership expires and depart two months later.

Whatever the disadvantages, the booking agents have their place. Even though I now consider myself to be an air courier veteran, I still use booking agents. One reason is their level of service. Now Voyager, for example, has a recorded message listing currently available flights and fares. (See the "International Air Courier Directory" for complete details.) Even though I can call without paying the registration fee (and know enough about the industry to be able to guess which companies are offering the flights listed), I view their recorded message, which is updated daily, as a "value-added" service which merits my continued loyalty as a consumer. The other booking agents in New York tell me they have plans to institute their own recorded information lines.

Naturally enough, the time may come when you will want to or have to deal directly with the air courier companies themselves. There are a number of reasons for this:

* It may be the only way to get where you want to go. The booking agencies don't provide universal coverage. For example, if you want to fly from New York to San Juan, you will have to deal directly with Rush Courier. Sometimes you will find that none of the booking agencies have a flight open when you want to go but a wholesaler does. Some of the destinations out of Miami are unreachable (as an air courier) from any other city; if you want to go, you will have to deal directly with one of the companies listed in the Directory.

* It's fun! There's no quicker or better way to feel like an air courier insider than to deal on a first-name basis with the courier companies themselves, talking the lingo, and getting inside information from the horse's mouth. Once you develop a personal relationship — and a track record for reliability and professionalism — you may even be able to move to the front of the line for special breaks such as last-minute bargain fares. (See Chapter Eight, "The Avid Courier," for more details,)

* You gain flexibility. If you travel frequently, as I do, you will soon find the limitations of the booking agents are "cramping your style." When you deal directly with the various air courier companies, *as well as* the booking agents, the whole world is accessible.

37

- It can be cheaper. Let's face it. We're talking bargain travel here, and the booking agents will mark up the fares, even if only a little bit. And if you don't have to pay a $50 fee, why do it?

If and when you decide to deal directly with an air courier company, you can simply use the "International Air Courier Directory" in Part II of this book to put yourself in touch with the companies that travel where you want to go.

Once you have an idea of where you want to go, when you want to go there, and the strategy you are going to use to get there, it's time to book your flight and take off. In the next chapter, I will walk you through the entire process, from the first phone call to your safe return home.

Chapter Four

How Air Courier Travel Works

E very air courier company has slightly different procedures but, in most cases, you can expect your air courier journey to unfold along these general lines:

Step 1: Booking your flight

I have yet to come across a courier company or booking agent that won't let you book a flight by phone. Simply call and say, "Hi. I'd like to go to Rio in June. What's available," and they'll tell you. In many respects, it's just like booking through any travel agent — with one important difference.

The courier company wants to lock in that booking as quickly as possible. to assure themselves that they have a courier for that flight. That means you will have to pay for your trip as soon as possible. The seat is not officially yours until you pay and a delay in paying may mean losing the ticket.

Some companies will hold your reservation for a non-refundable deposit, pending full payment by a certain number of days before departure. If there is a comfortable length of time before the flight you may be able to pay by a personal check through the mail. A few companies even take credit cards (which may add several percent to the cost of your ticket). Far more common are policies that require payment in cash or by certified check as soon as possible. That can mean showing up in person or sending payment by overnight mail. The "International Air Courier Directory" in Part II will help you determine which companies have which policies.

Once you have booked and secured a flight, you will most likely be asked to sign a contract. At this time, the company will make sure that you meet the minimum requirements (are 18 or 21 years of age, have a valid passport, don't have a spiked, day-glo hair-do and safety pins through your cheeks, and so forth). Sometimes all the contract-signing can be handled by fax. In some cases, you won't be asked to sign anything until you are being checked aboard your flight. We'll talk more about what you are agreeing to in these contracts in Chapter Seven, "Your Rights and Responsibilities."

Step 2: Boarding your flight

It's important to remember that, in the words of IBC, "you are not buying a ticket, but a trip." Even though your name may be on it, the ticket, technically, belongs to the air courier company. It's a subtle distinction that gives the courier company the right to "bump" you from the flight at the last minute. It does happen, but infrequently.

Another result is that you will not receive the actual ticket until shortly before the flight. The day before the flight, you will most likely be required to check in by phone; they want to make sure you're still "on" for the trip. On the day of the flight, well before your scheduled departure time (two or three hours), you will meet a representative of the courier company at a pre-arranged location in the airport — or, less frequently, at the courier company's offices. Some companies will ask you to phone in when you get to the airline terminal.

Arriving at the airport with no ticket, often with rather vague instructions on where to meet someone you have never laid eyes on, is a new experience for most travelers. Frankly it can be a little nerve-wracking.

I once called American Airlines on the day of a courier flight to see if I could have my Advantage number entered into their computer only to be told that my reservation had been cancelled. A call to the courier company brought reassurance that everything would be alright — as, indeed, it was.

Another common occurrence is to show up on time for your rendezvous with the courier rep only to be kept waiting for an hour or more. I now make it a point to bring with me the phone number of the courier company so I can call in if the rep is too long overdue. They always show up it seems. Any delays are caused by wanting to wait until the last possible minute to get as much cargo checked in as possible. So far — knock wood — I have never been left in the lurch at the airport and I have never heard of this happening to any other courier.

When the courier company rep arrives, you will be handed a one-way ticket to your destination, an envelope, usually sealed, containing the cargo manifests for the shipment you will accompany, and a sheet of instructions telling you what to do for the return flight.

The courier company representative will make sure that you are booked on the flight and get your boarding pass. In some cases, the rep will leave you in a waiting area and go deal with the ticket agents without you having to be present. At the very least, the

41

courier company representative will be at your elbow as you go through the check-in procedure.

The same is true of the shipment you are accompanying. Many times you will never see the shipment you are accompanying; other times, the courier company rep will check in the pouches at the same time you are checked in. The closest I've ever gotten to an air courier shipment was watching a burly young man drag four large, heavy, corrugated plastic bags full of smaller parcels to the weighing machine at the airline counter, while I stood by. You will be given the airline luggage check stubs for the courier shipment which you will have to surrender to the courier representative at your destination.

You will most likely be given something to help you identify yourself to the rep at the other end. One English company asks you to fill out a short questionnaire describing your dress and physical appearance; this is then faxed to the receiving company. Generally, your manifest envelope will serve as your identification. These are usually large, white, plastic envelopes with the courier company name or "ON-BOARD COURIER POUCH" emblazoned on them. Some companies issue their couriers with colored lapel pins or laminated, clip-on plastic ID tags, similar to those worn by airport personnel.

Your major responsibility en route is to keep the manifests, the baggage claim stubs, and your instruction sheet safe and secure about your person. Hardly an onerous task.

Step 3: Arriving at your destination

When you arrive at your destination, you will be met by another representative of the air courier company. You may have been instructed to hold up the envelope containing the manifests as you leave the customs area to identify you to the person meeting your flight. Sometimes you will be given a phone number to call when you have cleared through customs. (Usually you will breeze through customs by following the "Nothing To Declare" signs.)

Once you have made contact with the receiving courier company, you will be asked to wait — in the customs area of the terminal or in a building elsewhere on the airport grounds — while the courier company representative walks the paperwork and the checked baggage through the customs process. Once that's done, you'll be free to leave.

In my experience, this has been a hassle-free experience. I have, however, seen other couriers who were not so lucky. While I was leaving after a five-minute wait at the courier shed in London, a courier from an earlier flight was fuming that he'd been kept waiting for hours with no explanation about the cause of the delay. On other trips to London, I haven't even been required to go to the customs shed; the rep simply asked where they could get in touch with me if they had to and let me go.

Once through customs, you are on your own, free to do and see as you please until the return flight.

Step 4: Returning home

I have found that one of the most important documents I carry as a courier is the instruction sheet for my return flight. By all means, keep this document in a safe place. I copy the key information — return flight number and date, contact name, and phone numbers — onto several different pieces of paper to stash in various wallets and shirt pockets, just in case.

Usually, you will be asked to check in by phone with the local office of the air courier company the day before your return flight to confirm your flight and pick up any last minute instructions or

43

changes in plan. In some countries, this can be a challenge, especially if you are not in the city in which the office is located. Believe me, you will complain far less about American phone companies once you have tried repeatedly and unsuccessfully to make a long distance call from a provincial city to the capital of a foreign country. Plan accordingly.

And don't forget to call or think it's just a formality that can be skipped. I have had flight times, even airlines, switched at the last minute. So always remember to check in. At the very least, failure to check in will earn a black mark by your name in the courier company's records.

On the day of your return flight, the arrangements are a mirror image of the routine on the flight out — meet the representative at the airport, receive the manifests, get checked in, receive your ticket, board the flight, meet the representative back in New York, or Los Angeles, or London. Most courier company reps will speak English, but you cannot always expect your foreign contact to speak, let alone be fluent in, English, especially in Latin America. A few pleasantries in the local language will come in handy. Fortunately, unless you have some problem, the procedure is so cut-and-dried that not being able to speak the language won't be a handicap.

That's all there is to it. Considering how much you save on your fare, it's extremely well-paid "employment."

C an things go wrong? Of course they can, but they're the same problems that plague any other air traveler — delayed or cancelled flights, overbookings, missed connections, and so forth.

Sometimes the glitches in a courier trip can be more interesting than inconvenient. David Bogartz had just such an experience on a trip to Oslo. "The representative meeting me there asked me to help him take the freight off the conveyor belt," he told me. "Being a nice guy, I couldn't say no, so together we dragged the bags out to the sidewalk. I could see through the plastic shells that the contents were Airborne Express packages. I wonder what the Airborne customers would think if they knew a computer programmer from Cambridge, Mass., had been dragging them across Fornebu Airport?"

On other occasions, the glitches can be more irksome. "I was going from Los Angeles to Singapore," recalls long-time courier George Sprague. "I was dropping off some baggage in Seoul and then going on. Now normally, you hand the claim checks to [the courier company's] representative and he takes care of everything. In Seoul, it's a little different; in Seoul, the courier is responsible for getting the stuff through customs and then handing it over to the representative.

"So it's Sunday night, it's winter, it's ten degreees below zero, I'm dressed for Singapore, I have 2,000 pounds of baggage, and the people who were supposed to meet me never showed up. Of course, they close Seoul airport at midnight and I have no place to put the baggage and no hotel. They were supposed to take me into town and put me up in a hotel.

"So I got customs to let me throw all the stuff back in the baggage area and I got my own hotel. I had all the tickets, so the next morning I caught my flight to Singapore and they didn't get their baggage in time." In spite of the hassle, George remained philosophical. "Screw ups are possible," he notes.

And sometimes the "problems" can be downright wonderful. Journalist Lee Solomon claims to have "the best courier story ever," and she just may be right. On her very first courier experience she booked a last-minute flight via Pan Am from New York to Frankfort. The $150 fare was good enough but things quickly got better.

Courier companies like to be the last to check baggage for a flight. That way they can accommodate last-minute packages. On Lee's flight, she and a courier for another company weren't put on the flight until the economy section had completely filled. The result was that they were both bumped up to First Class. While sipping champagne over the Atlantic, Lee was handed a scratch-off game ticket as part of Pan Am's fiftieth anniversary celebration.

"I won a free round-trip to anywhere in the world," Lee recalls. "Then, when I went to India on my free trip, they credited my frequent flyer mileage twice which meant that, with the mileage I got for going to Frankfort, I was eligible for another free trip which I'm going to use to go to Africa. I wound up getting three trips, all for $150!"

Chapter Five

How Cheap Is Cheap?

The big attraction of traveling as an air courier, of course, is the tremendous discounts off the regular coach fares that come as part of the territory. The ticketed price of my first round-trip to London, which I described earlier, was $920; I paid just $250 and I booked the flight less than a week in advance. Of course, if I had booked well in advance for a super-saver fare I might have been able to do better than $920, but no airline, to my knowledge, offers a $250 round-trip fare to London.

Charter fares tend to be more competitive with courier travel but are still priced higher, sometimes much higher, than the fares cited in this guide. What's more, charters are notoriously unreliable. Courier flights, however, are on regularly scheduled airlines. Even in the unlikely event that a flight is cancelled, your ticket guarantees you passage on the next available flight out.

To give you an idea of what you can expect to save as a courier, you will find, on the next page, a chart listing flights and fares that might be offered out of New York, by one booking agent, in the middle of the summer, when fares are at their highest.

This listing offers several impressive bargains. Madrid, at $150 RT, has been marked down from an earlier $399 fare. The reason?

DATE: July 14th

Destination	Date	Length of Stay	Fare
Amsterdam	7/27	1 week	$399
Brussels	8/4	1 week	$399
Buenos Aires	7/25	8 days	$399
Caracas	8/14	1 week	$175
Copenhagen	7/17	1 week	$199
Frankfort	7/27	1 week	$399
Helsinki	7/19	1 week	$199
Hong Kong	9/6	1 week to 30 days	$599
London	8/28	1 week	$350
London	9/7	up to 30 days	$399
London (from Houston)	7/26	up to 30 days	$375
Madrid	7/16	1 week	$150
Mexico City	7/25	1 week	$99
Mexico City	7/24	up to 3 months	$125
Milan	9/13	2 weeks	$399
Paris	7/19	2 weeks	$199
Rio	9/26	8 days	$399
Rome	9/4	8 days	$399
Santiago	8/15	13 days	$399
Seoul	7/20	2 weeks	$575
Singapore	N/A		
Stockholm	8/22	1 week	$299
Tokyo	N/A		
Zurich	8/14	1 week	$399

Check the dates; the flight leaves in two days. Even in the off-season, the generally available courier fares to Madrid are $299. Compare this to the $1,520 unrestricted coach fare you'd have to pay if you wanted to fly on the spur of the moment. That means this discounted courier flight is one-tenth the regular coach fare. Even with a 14-day advance purchase, with restrictions, the cheapest flight to Madrid would set you back $776 for a mid-week departure. So, flying as a courier, you're paying one-fifth (or 19.23%) of the cheapest fare.

Other bargain flights leaving in a few days are Helsinki at $199 (down from $250), Copenhagen at $199 (down from $299), and Paris, a super bargain, at $199 for two weeks (down from $399). Another eye-opener on this list is the Mexico City fares. The fare had been running at $125 for a one week stay. Here a one week stay is $99 and a three month stay is available for $125.

Even at "full" fares, courier travel offers significant savings. The Milan and Rome fares listed above correspond to Alitalia's cheapest fares for the same dates of $870 and $920 respectively. So even the highest fares you will pay as a courier on these routes are less than half what you could get from an airline. Or, for the mathematically minded, 43% and 46% respectively.

While we're at it, the above list also illustrates some other aspects of courier travel. The earliest flight available on the date listed was two days away; the latest was just over nine weeks away. That's fairly typical of the industry, regardless of where you book your flights, although some flights can be booked as much as three months in advance.

Another thing you'll notice is that not all the destinations usually offered by this booking agent were available on this particular day. It's impossible to predict, much less guarantee, what will be available through any air courier contact when you call. Of course, you might be able to call another booking agent or an air courier company directly and find additional flights or better fares. As an example, while this booking agent was offering $399 flights to Milan, it was possible to find a $300 fare through a retailer.

Perhaps most important to the avid traveler is the fact that, on this particular date (and this doesn't change throughout the year), a wide variety of destinations and departure dates was available. Whether you want to leave quickly to wherever the Fates may dictate or want to be choosy and wait for the "right" destination, you will always be able to book a flight and still save hundreds of dollars — money that can be better spent doing what you want to do where you want to do it.

In some respects, courier fares directly mirror standard air fares. That is, they tend to be higher during the summer and during holiday periods and cheaper during the so-called off-season. In one important respect, however, courier fares behave precisely the opposite of those offered by the airlines.

The farther away the flight date the better deal you can get on a "regular" fare from the airlines. As the flight date approaches, the few special promotional seats being sold at attractive "come-on" prices get filled. Next the 21 or 14 day advance purchase dates pass by. Finally, if you are forced to fly at short notice, the airlines sock it to you with their "unrestricted" coach fares, which can be truly astronomical, especially if you are not used to being forced to pay them.

For couriers the opposite is true. When the flight is still months away, the courier company will charge what they think the traffic will bear. As the flight date approaches, however, they begin to get nervous. The airlines can send a plane out with empty seats but the courier company has only one seat to fill and fill it they must. Within a week or two of flight time, the fares begin to drop.

So, if you can travel on the spur of the moment (and aren't too fussy about the destination), you can have the best of all possible worlds. As it gets closer to flight time, most companies lower the fare dramatically. I have seen Copenhagen for $50, Zurich for $99, and Buenos Aires for $199. And remember, those are round-trip fares! Times of international turmoil, like the Gulf War, are another harbinger of bargain fares. During that period you could find $99 round-trip fares to much of Europe and in some cases could even book a month or more in advance.

But wait! It gets better. When it gets *really* close to flight time, the courier companies begin to get desperate. Now Voyager once offered a chance to fly to Hong Kong for free. Shortly before this book went to press, Discount Travel International gave away a trip to Zurich. Jupiter Air, in San Francisco, and IBC-Pacific, in Los Angeles, are courier companies that will sometimes waive the fare for the last-minute traveler who helps them out of a bind. Obviously, because of the short fuse on last-minute bargains, they require that you be in or close to the city of departure.

In the "International Air Courier Directory", I alert you to those companies that have established procedures for alerting you to last-minute bargain fares and free flights, but the same principle applies to any courier company. If a courier isn't available for a flight, the cargo still has to go, and the owner of the company may not be as eager to go to Hong Kong or Rio as you or I.

Just because a flight is last-minute does not invariably mean that it will be free. Some companies seem to have firm policies on always charging something, no matter how short-notice the trip. You can always hold out for a lower fare or no fare, of course. The courier company may have other people on its list, however, and know that if you won't pay the price they ask, the next person they call, or the next, will.

If you are flexible as to your destination, I wouldn't worry about finding a bargain flight at the last minute — at least from New York. I regularly monitor the availability of flights. The longest time lag I have found between the date I call and the date of the next available flight is three days. In such a situation, don't hesitate to suggest a lower fare if it hasn't already been lowered.

You will find more on the subject of last-minute flights and bargain fares in Chapter Eight, "The Avid Courier."

A ll talk of "free" courier flights should be taken with just a grain of salt. Just as there's no such thing as a free lunch, there's no such thing as an absolutely free courier trip. At the very least you will have to pay the applicable departure taxes (see below). Which is another way of saying that you will never travel for the fare the courier companies quote you.

One "hidden" cost has already been mentioned — the fees some booking agents charge. If you pay $50 annually and fly twice you have added $25 to the cost of each flight. When dealing with the already low cost of courier travel, this added expense is noticeable if not exactly onerous.

You may also incur some expenses in booking and paying for your flight. If you live in Las Vegas, Nevada, or Glasgow,

Scotland, you will ring up some long distance charges before your flight is booked. If the time is short, you may find yourself paying to send and receive faxes of contracts. Banks will charge you for a certified check; money orders also cost money, although generally less than bank fees. Overnight mail or FedEx costs can also be a significant expense, especially if the courier fare is low.

Another fact of travel (and life in general) is taxes. The "good news" here is that you don't pay any more than anyone else on your flight. Nor do you pay any less. On a trip I took to Caracas for $175 round-trip, I paid a $16 departure tax in New York and another $11 departure tax in Caracas. That added just over 15% to the effective cost of my fare. Out of San Francisco to the Orient, the departure tax is $36.

Some companies require a refundable deposit of from $100 to $500 to "encourage" you to make the return flight. If you miss that flight — even if you have the best "excuse" in the world — you lose that deposit. Whenever I travel outside the city in which I land on a courier flight, I make it a steadfast policy to get back at least the day before my return flight. That way if I have any problems — cancelled internal flights, lost travelers checks, illness, or whatever — I have some built in slack to maximize my chances of making that return flight.

Once you return, you will have to reclaim your deposit. This can often involve making a personal visit to the courier company or making cumbersome arrangements to reclaim your money through the mail.

Even if you make your return flight and get your deposit back, you lose the "opportunity value" of your money — that is, the interest you'd have earned if you'd left it in your savings account. If you used a money order (a common form of payment), you also paid a dollar or two in fees. Instead, see if you can put your deposit on a credit card slip; they only submit the bill if you forfeit your deposit. (Yes, yes, I know this is picky stuff, but if you're not interested in saving money, why are you reading this book?) Some companies will encourage you, once they have your deposit, to leave it with them. That way, they argue, you won't have to worry about making the deposit on your next flight. You will have to decide whether this small convenience is worth giving the company a long-term, interest-free loan. If you're like me, inertia can play a role too. I left a return deposit sitting with a courier company on the theory that I'd have use for it in the not-too-far-distant future. That was two years ago — I've just never gotten around to using it because I've been flying with other companies.

Then, of course, there is the always inflated cost of getting to the airport. For those of you who may be leaving from New York, let me pass along the following low-cost method for getting from Manhattan to Kennedy Airport (JFK).

Take the Rockaway bound "A" train to the Howard Beach/JFK stop. Be careful! One version of the "A" train goes to Lefferts Boulevard. You may also take the "C" train between 6 a.m. and 9 p.m. Sometimes (after midnight, for example) you will have to switch from the "A" to the "H" train at Euclid Avenue for service to the Howard Beach/JFK stop. Once on the "A" train it's a good idea to ask the conductor or a passenger to make sure. And, yes, New Yorkers can be both friendly and helpful! At the Howard Beach stop you can board a free 24-hour shuttle service to the JFK terminals. Total fare: $1.15.

Since you will only be toting carry-on baggage, this alternative over a taxi ($30 or more) or the bus ($11 to $12.50) is well worth it. Budget at least two hours from midtown Manhattan to make the trip.

Another "extra" (but not necessarily inevitable) cost of courier travel is excess baggage, which I will discuss in the next chapter.

Courier companies are not travel agents. They provide only your transportation from a gateway city to and from the destination you have chosen. If you don't live in or near one of the "gateway" cities listed in the "International Air Courier Directory", you must find some way of getting there for your flight. What you do and where you stay once you get to your destination are completely up to you. Don't expect any help from the courier company on booking land accommodations. You may want to turn to a travel agent for help; just be aware of the fact that the agent may not react kindly to the news that you have already booked your flight.

An exception to this rule is Focus on Travel in San Francisco (see the "International Air Courier Directory"). Because they handle the purchasing of tickets for IBC-Pacific's courier routes, they are a logical choice for hotel reservations in the Orient. Be sure to identify yourself as an IBC courier when you call. If you want to use a travel agent for land arrangements on other routes, tell the courier company what you have in mind and ask them which agent handles their ticket purchases.

It is also generally true that the courier company cannot help you get from Kansas City to a flight that leaves from Los Angeles or Miami. One exception is the booking agency Courier Travel Service in New York. I have heard that they have been very helpful in booking out-of-town couriers on connecting flights into New York.

For those of you who do not live in or near a gateway city, the

55

additional cost of transportation is a genuine concern. Fortunately, there are a number of strategies you can use to keep your in-country costs down. One option is to plan your courier travel around a business trip to a gateway city. That way, you will at least be able to deduct the cost of the domestic travel from your income tax.

Or, in the spirit of ultra-low-cost travel you may want to look into a "drive-away" to get you to your port of embarkation. Check your Yellow Pages under "Automobile Transporters and Drive-Away Companies" for outfits that will let you drive a car that needs to be delivered where you are going. The cities from which courier flights leave are popular destinations and you may be able to make the trip for little more than the cost of gas.

If you don't have the time to drive, you can either plan far enough in advance to qualify for advance-purchase discount fares or seek out some of the low-cost domestic air fare alternatives.

Another option is to dip into your reserve of frequent flyer miles to get a free round-trip ticket to a gateway city. Anyone who travels regularly on business is enrolled in at least one airline program. Increasingly, you don't even have to fly to earn mileage credit.

American Airlines, for example, offers a number of ways to earn frequent flyer mileage credit without ever boarding a plane. If you use MCI for your long-distance telephone calls, you can enroll in a program which ties your long-distance bill into American's AAdvantage program. Call (800) 999-1909 to enroll and receive a 500 mile bonus just for signing up. Once you are registered, you will receive five AAdvantage miles for every dollar of long distance calls you make with MCI. Of course, if you don't use MCI, you can always switch.

You may also apply for a Visa or MasterCard from Citibank that gives you one mile of AAdvantage frequent flyer credit for each dollar you charge. The annual fee is $50, with the usual stiff annual interest. To apply by phone call (800) 359-4444. Both American Express and Diners Club offer similar programs that have the additional advantage of allowing you to gain frequent flyer credit with a number of airlines.

Take a moment to reread the rules of the frequent flyer programs in which you are enrolled. Most of them have "partners"—hotels and car rental agencies — which allow you to accumulate additional mileage credit. Simply switching hotels on your domestic travels may earn you enough mileage to fly free to a courier gateway.

If you don't have enough of your own frequent flyer miles, consider buying someone else's. Check the classifieds in your local newspapers for people selling tickets or frequent flyer bonuses they can't use. *USA Today* regularly carries classified ads of companies that specialize in in this business. Make sure you know the "retail price" of the ticket you want and be prepared to negotiate aggressively for the lowest fare.

Consolidators, as they are known in the airline business, deserve special mention. In the simplest terms, a consolidator is a travel specialist who buys wholesale and sells below retail. In this case, the commodity being purchased is airplane seats. Consolidators buy large blocks of seats from the airlines at steep discounts. They then turn around and sell those seats to you or me at a price that is well below the ticket's "face value" but still high enough to earn them a profit.

When considering travel from a gateway city, consolidators can't come close to beating courier fares, as the following head-to-head comparison illustrates. All fares quoted are round-trip; where more than one fare is given, the consolidator quoted different fares for different airlines. The fares quoted are for the same dates of travel and length of stay.

Route	Courier	Consolidator
LA-Taipei	$300 (IBC-Pacific)	$755 - $795 (Euro-Asia Express)
NY-Hong Kong	$450 (Now Voyager)	$890 (RMC)
NY-Milan	$200 (World)	$678 - $738 (Ameropa)
NY-London	$250 (Now Voyager)	$586 (Moment's Notice)
Miami-Rio	$350 (Line Haul)	$822 (25 Travel)
Chicago-Mexico City	$200 (Leisure Mktg)	$327 - $343 (Mena)

If you're leaving from London, consolidator fares tend to be much more competitive with courier fares, although they are invariably higher by £50 to £100. If you are based in England, you may find that the extra cost may be worth it to you, especially if the alternative is not making the trip. You will find a longer discussion of England's consolidators in the "International Air Courier Directory" in Part II.

If you don't live near a gateway city, however, consolidators may offer an attractive alternative. For example, there are many flights from Atlanta to Europe but (to my knowledge) no courier flights. A consolidator may be able to quote you a fare that is competitive with the cost of flying to New York or Miami to connect with a Europe-bound courier flight.

Generally speaking, consolidators offer overseas flights only, although a number deal with domestic flights as well. Those that do tend to offer long-haul routes (New York - LA, LA - Miami) or trips to Hawaii. In other words, if you live in Kansas City you'll have better luck asking a consolidator to get you to Hong Kong or Frankfort than to Los Angeles or Miami.

Another alternative is to call Airhitch. Airhitch (which has offices in New York and Los Angeles and which is listed in the "International Air Courier Directory") is not a consolidator but a specialist in space-available travel. While most of the flights they offer leave from New York and L.A., they sometimes have flights leaving from other locations.

A Special Report, *Consolidators — Air Travel's Bargain Basement*, is available from Inwood Training Publications for $4.00. This report lists scores of consolidators throughout the United States that let you book by phone and receive your tickets in the mail. For more information, see *Resources for the Intrepid Traveler*, at the back of this book.

Finally, you might want to keep an eye peeled for special deals and promotional fares available from the airlines themselves. I have never seen these fares match courier fares but sometimes they get close. For example, as the second edition was going to press here were some deals being offered by various airlines:

• To inaugurate its Philadelphia to Paris service, USAir was promoting a $318 round-trip fare for mid-week departures; the fare was $368 for weekend departures.

- Icelandair was offering round-trips to Luxembourg from New York and Baltimore for $398 and from Orlando for $498, with a free rental car for a week (if two people traveled together).

- Virgin Atlantic was pushing a "Late Latesaver" fare from Boston to London for $179 one way or $368 round-trip, which would make it very competitive with a New York courier flight if you lived in or near Boston.

All of these alternatives have attractions for those living near the departure cities or for people who want to travel together.

How do you find out about these special deals? Good question. It can be difficult. I subscribe to *Consumer Reports Travel Letter*, which alerts subscribers to opportunities like this and from which the above examples were drawn. Trouble is, these promotional fares are often sold out before the newsletter arrives. Perhaps the best way to monitor the availability of specials like these is to find a good travel agent who will tip you off when a too-good-to-pass-up opportunity comes along.

Chapter Six

Tradeoffs

❝ ❝I f it sounds too good to be true, it probably is." While that may be overstating the case a bit, there are some tradeoffs to air courier travel.

The biggest drawback, from the point of view of most people I've talked to about air courier travel, is the baggage limitation. You are limited to one piece of carry-on luggage, so if you haven't mastered the art of traveling light, courier travel may be a bit of a challenge.

Before I became an air courier, I was an inveterate over-packer— the sort of person who'd throw in a tuxedo "just in case." As it happened, I found the discipline of reducing all my travel needs to a single bag strangely liberating. I have now arrived at the point where I find I am *still* over-packing, even in just one carry-on bag!

Another "advantage" of traveling light, I have discovered, is that even on a one week trip you will most likely have to do some laundry. Of course, you can send it out, if you are staying in a hotel that offers laundry service. I prefer to do it myself. Going to the laundramat may be an unwelcome chore at home, but in Rome or Buenos Aires, it becomes an enjoyable cross-cultural adventure!

Actually, what constitutes "carry-on baggage" is a matter of constantly shifting definition. Some courier companies specify you may only take one bag, while others allow you two. The airlines, for their part, have their own definitions. The "standard" definition is *one* bag with combined dimensions (length, width, and height) that do not exceed 45 inches and that does not weigh more than 70 pounds. Generally, the less crowded the flight, the more you can get away with as carry-on baggage. The key factor is that whatever you lug aboard fit in the overhead compartment or underneath your seat.

I have taken to traveling with two bags — one is a largish leather bag which just meets the airlines' combined height, width, and length requirements. The other is a small, over-the-shoulder bag in which I carry camera, guide books, tickets, and so forth. I have never been challenged and have never found the combination a burden.

If you absolutely can't stuff everything you need into one little bag, you might consider wearing several layers of clothing. Women, of course, have the option of carrying an oversized "purse" in addition to their regular carry-on allotment.

As a last resort, you can simply pack another bag and pay the airline for "excess baggage." If you do this, make sure you check with the airline for the prices and procedures on the route you are flying *before you get to the airport.* Policies vary greatly from airline to airline and from route to route, in part due to regulations mandated by the country to which you will be flying. For example, TWA allows you to take any number of extra bags on its New York to Paris flights for $70 each; the bags may not exceed 100 inches in total dimension or weigh more than 100 pounds. On American's Miami to Guatemala route, on the other hand, you are limited to one excess bag (no boxes) not to exceed 80 inches in total dimension and no more than 70 pounds for the comparatively modest fee of $35. If the bag exceeds either requirement, the cost jumps to $70.

Sometimes the problem is not what you want to take with you but what you want to carry back. If you plan on doing any heavy shopping, my advice would be to make as many arrangements as possible for shipping it back before you leave. The embassy or consulate of the country in question will direct you to reputable shipping companies. Another good source of information about reputable shippers and procedures is the American Chamber of Commerce, which can be found in most major foreign cities.

And don't put off your shopping spree until the last minute. I once had to pass up some fabulous bargains in Mexico City because the merchant didn't ship to the United States and I had no time to make other arrangements.

Be aware, too, that on some courier runs you will be either going or returning "empty" — that is, there will be no courier pouches to accompany on one leg of the trip. Sometimes, this is a peculiarity of that particular route, other times it's simply the luck of the draw. If it's important to you, ask about it before your trip. If you know you'll be returning empty, you can plan on bringing a collapsible bag with you and loading up on goodies while overseas.

Another drawback of courier travel is that you will most likely travel alone. Invariably, any given company has one courier seat on any given flight. Sometimes it may be possible to book seats on succeeding days. Use the "International Air Courier Directory" to spot likely candidates for this arrangement.

Or you can simply tell the courier company what you have in mind when you call. Companies that offer several flights a week are the most obvious choices. If they can swing it, they'll be more than happy to accommodate you. After all, they need to fill those seats.

Obviously, the farther in advance you book the better your odds of booking on successive days. Discount Travel International of New York tells me they are regularly able to accommodate couples with this type of arrangement. Before you dismiss this strategy out of hand, consider the benefits. Most couples do not share all the same interests; there are invariably sights to see and things to do that appeal to one more than the other. This strategy gives each person some time on their own at the destination to use as they see fit, without worrying about boring their companion.

If you simply can't bear to be separated, there are other options. With a little advance planning, you should have no trouble booking a super-saver fare for a companion on your courier flight.

It is also theoretically possible (although I've never tried it) to find two different courier companies with seats on the same flight or at least on the same day to the same destination. Your best chance for this kind of arrangement is on the heavily traveled London - New York corridor. The only courier run I know of on which you can regularly book two seats on the same plane is the New York to Madrid route offered through Halbart and several booking agencies.

In general, however, air courier travel works best for the solo traveler. Which may not be as bad as it sounds. Even the most social among us sometimes has a need to get away by themselves. If you've been promising yourself that some day you'll "do" the Louvre, or if you want to go snorkeling on a tiny coral island in the Caribbean, or simply want to "stand silent on a peak in

Darien," a courier flight may be just the ticket.

It is often said in the industry that the air courier must be flexible. Yet, paradoxically, you also lose flexibility. You must fit yourself into the company's schedule, not vice versa. While you can pick your destination, it is not always possible to pick your dates. And sometimes you can pick the date, if you are willing to be "flexible" on the destination.

Once a flight is booked, the dates are locked in. Most courier companies have fixed lengths of stay for each route. For them, it's purely a matter of convenience. It's a lot easier to keep things organized if you know that every courier returns in precisely one week, than if you have to juggle lengths of stay ranging from a few days to several months.

Other companies will offer flexible stays "up to 21 days" or "up to a month." That does not always means that you can pick any length of stay within that time frame. More likely, your date of return will have to coincide with an available flight.

Some companies will try to accommodate requests. For example, if the usual stay at a particular destination is two weeks and someone wants to stay only one week, that might be arranged if someone else is willing to stay three. These special arrangements are rare, however.

The rigid length of stay requirements also mean that you can forget about changing your return date. You may fall in love with Paris or Rio but if you want to spend more time there, you'll have to plan another trip. Don't think you can talk the courier company into letting you stay and extra few days. Still, special circumstances do arise and — who knows — it may just be in the company's interests to have you stay an extra month. As with so much else in life, it never hurts to ask.

But in spite of the drawbacks — and there's no point pretending they don't exist — air courier travel, because of its very unpredictability, remains one of the few real adventures left in this age of homogenized travel. If you've never traveled on a whim, being an air courier will give you the experience of taking off at short notice to points unknown. If you've written off the Far East or South America as vacation destinations because they're just too far away and too expensive, air courier travel can make these exotic destinations suddenly affordable.

I especially recommend air courier travel to people who, like me once-upon-a-time, used to plan their vacations down to the nth detail. Dropping everything after a job well done or at the tell-tale signs of burnout and saying, "The heck with it. I need a break," then picking up the phone and saying, "I'm ready to go. What's available?" is one of the most liberating experiences imaginable.

Try it. It's worked wonders for me. It can for you, too.

Chapter Seven

Your Rights and Responsibilities

T he question I am asked most frequently about my courier travels is, "How do you know you're not transporting drugs?" It's gotten to be a bit of a joke.

The fact is that the courier business is as boring as most other businesses. Things get moved from Point A to Point B and if someone, somewhere along the line, slips some contraband into a shipment, it's certainly not your fault. As the folks at IBC told me, "the individual shipments are inspected prior to being manifested so that only legal commodities are being shipped."

It also helps to remember that most of the material you will be accompanying is being sent by companies with whom the courier companies have long-standing business relationships. In the lingo of the airlines, these are "known shippers." It is relatively rare that a stranger to the courier company walks in with a single package to ship. In any event, all packages, suspicious or not, are x-rayed by the courier company before they are trucked to the airport.

The people in customs know this as well. In fact, I have received far less attention from American customs when arriving as a courier than I ever did when arriving as a regular "tourist." Also, the last time I returned from London, I carried a letter from the London courier firm stating in black and white that I had no personal responsibility for the contents of the shipment I was accompanying. Needless to say, I didn't have to flash it in self-defence.

In the unlikely event that some contraband does turn up in a shipment you are accompanying, the suspicion will fall not on you, not on the courier company, but on the person who sent the package originally. You probably wouldn't be inconvenienced in any case since you most likely would have left the airport before any contraband was detected.

The non-issue of drug smuggling aside, the fact remains that being a courier is a serious business that involves a contractual relationship between you and the company for which you are serving as a courier. Each of you has mutual obligations which are spelled out in the agreement you sign before traveling.

To state the obvious, I am not a lawyer and it is certainly not my intention to render any legal advice. This chapter contains only the ruminations of a layperson. Should you feel the need for legal counsel before embarking on a courier trip, by all means seek it. Just don't seek it here.

One of the more curious aspects of courier travel is that the courier companies will insist (in the fine print of their contracts) that your ticket is free; then they turn around and cheerfully charge you for that "free" ticket. "The airplane passenger ticket to and/or from your courier destination is free of charge in consideration of your performance of JUPITER non-salaried On board Courier duties," says Jupiter's contract. But several paragraphs later the contract stipulates, "There is an administrative charge of _____ payable at the time the offer is accepted. The administrative charge serves to cover part of JUPITER's related administrative and operational expenses and is not charged by JUPITER as an agent for any airlines or as a ticket agent." The blank space is filled in with the amount of whatever "fare" you have agreed to pay for your Jupiter flight.

To the courier, the money paid to the courier company looks, feels, and acts like a fare. In the "International Air Courier Directory" in this book, I always refer to the fees charged as fares. To normal folks like you and me they are fares.

To the lawyers who draft the contracts, however, there is a crucial difference. In their efforts to protect their clients (the air courier companies) from every possible eventuality, the legal eagles have set things up in such a way that the courier never has the actual, technical, legal ownership of the ticket. The courier company always retains ownership and control of the ticket, even if it has your name on it.

This arrangement offers the courier company the maximum flexibility. It enables them to change plans — or even cancel — at the last minute. Suppose, for example, that you have made arrangements with a courier company to be their courier on an American Airlines flight to London. At the last minute, they get a large rush shipment from a major customer, too late to make the American flight. However, they *can* get the shipment on a later Air India flight. If the ticket was "yours," you could say, "Tough. I want to go on American and collect my frequent flyer miles. This late shipment is your problem."

The way the contract you signed is written enables the courier company to cancel the flight on American and put you on the later Air India flight, frequent flyer miles or no.

Another common contractual provision is confidentiality. Halbart's contract, for example, asks you to agree to the following statement: "I will not discuss with anyone Halbart's method of operation or names or lists of clients of which I may be aware, or which may be in my possession."

I suppose that could be interpreted to mean that you couldn't tell the person sitting next to you on the plane that you paid a fraction of the going rate for your ticket in exchange for acting as a courier, although most couriers I have spoken with tell me that bragging about the fare they paid is one of the best things about courier travel.

According to Jonathon Steinberg, an international lawyer who represents several air courier companies, the confidentiality clause is meant to protect the companies from industrial espionage. If you traveled with a courier company on several trips, learned the ins and outs of their operation, picked up the names of some of their best customers, and then set up a courier company of your own, in direct competition, they would have some legal recourse.

C an you collect frequent flyer mileage when you travel as a courier?

The answer depends on who you talk to. Some courier companies will tell you that you can collect the mileage; they may even use that fact as an inducement for you to fly with them. Others will insist that it is impossible for couriers to collect frequent flyer credit.

My advice is to ask about frequent flyer mileage when you book your flight. If they say "no," ask the airline when you check in for your flight. Very often, they will take your frequent flyer number, even though the courier company has told you you're not eligible.

It's happened to me. While checking in for a courier flight from London, I handed my frequent flyer card to the ticketing agent. The courier company rep said, jokingly, that he thought the courier company should get the frequent flyer credit since, after all, it was the courier company that paid for the ticket. The ticketing agent disagreed. "It's the bloke what puts 'is bottom in the seat what gets the credit," he said. Amen.

There may be some situations in which you are really not eligible. In the past, for instance, courier companies would buy special, low-cost tickets which were coded by the airline's computers as ineligible for frequent flyer credit. These tickets are less common today and will be phased out completely in the near future I am told. Lawyer Steinberg, a frequent courier himself, suggests that, whatever the situation, you always ask for your frequent flyer miles. "Airline regulations and codes are so complex and in such a state of flux," he notes, "that very often the person doing the ticketing doesn't what what's allowed and what isn't."

Far and away the most important obligation you have as a courier is to be where you are supposed to be when you are supposed to be there. Carrying an envelope on an international flight is not exactly a job for a rocket scientist. However, making flight connections and following simple written instructions is something that, so I have been told, eludes a surprising number of would-be couriers.

Among the cardinal sins are missing flights or waltzing through customs without meeting the courier representative and turning over the manifest. Any such transgression means instant black-listing by the courier company involved and perhaps by others as well. In New York, for example, many courier companies turn over the job of handling incoming courier shipments to New York Air Courier Clearance (NYACC). A similar service is performed at London's Heathrow Airport by Courier Facilities Ltd. The people staffing these operations get so annoyed with less than responsible couriers that they are liable to spread the (bad) word among the companies they service.

Sometimes, the payback can be more immediate. A courier rep at Heathrow in London told me of a returning courier to New York who tried to avoid his responsibilities by telling the airline he had lost his ticket. Sure enough a check of the computer revealed a ticket in his name (paid for by the courier firm) and a new ticket was issued.

The courier rep, who was holding the real ticket, suspected something was amiss when the courier didn't show up as pre-arranged. He asked the ticket agents if Jim Smith (not his real name) had checked in and was told, "Yeah, that's him over there."

The rep approached Smith who admitted that he simply had wanted to save himself some time at customs in New York. The courier rep, predictably, was not amused. Jim Smith was now faced with a choice, lose his ticket and pay his own way home or complete his agreed-on mission as a courier. He chose the latter.

The London courier firm faxed a complete description of the

offending courier to New York along with a few nasty suggestions about how he might be best handled. The result: Jim Smith spent three long hours bottled up in customs before being released.

When you get right down to it, there's not a lot to do as a courier. You are simply operating as a very small cog in a much larger operation. Everything has been done to make your job as foolproof as possible — not so much for your benefit as for the company's

Once aboard, you are just another coach passenger. Your "job" as a courier earns you no special privileges or consideration — although a courier from Wales told me that on a flight from London to Philadelphia he talked the cabin attendant into letting him sit next to the door in Club Class "since I was carrying urgent courier documents." (How do you say 'chutzpah' in Welsh?)

Still, small though your part is, it is important. Carrying out your part of the bargain promptly and efficiently will help you build a reputation that can pay off down the road in inside information and special deals. It will also help remind the courier companies that freelancers can be a valuable and valued part of their operation.

Fortunately, most people who fly as freelance, on-board couriers are solid citizens who take their courier duties seriously, even if it means some discomfort. The following story was told me by a British courier who requested anonymity. He was on his first courier flight, from London to New York. Everything went smoothly, until he checked in for his return flight. Then came an announcement of a delay in the flight. Our courier picks up the tale:

"It was whilst I stood by the desk in the departure lounge that my problems began. I had thought it best to ask if I could phone [the courier company] to let them know about the delay. As I stood by the desk, waiting my turn to ask, a person with an official air appeared quickly by my side and said 'Courier?'

"Taken by surprise, I answered 'yes' and in my confusion allowed him to take the sheets of information that [the courier company] issues couriers and that gives telephone numbers in case of emergency. As he went to walk off with these I said, somewhat sternly, 'I'll keep the documentation,' and took a firm hold of them. For a split second we both held this sheet and my heart started to hammer. I thought he was not going to let go. 'We are both in the same business,' he said. 'I worked for [the airline] for 30 years and then I started playing around with this.' I kept a firm hold on the sheet as I asked him if he worked for [the courier company] but he zoomed off without, apparently, hearing me. After speaking to the desk staff, I found a wall to lean against and I saw this man again. He was in his sixties and reasonably smartly dressed in a brown sports jacket and trousers. He started to fiddle with one of the computer terminals at the desks and when an airport employee walked up to see what he was doing he used the same attitude that he had used on me and the employee walked away. I was not so convinced and wondered if he was some type of con-man.

"Much later, on the way to the hotel, the airplane unfixable until the morning, I saw him again. He showed me a telex that he had sent out which advised his family that he would be late. I was impressed but still deeply suspicious. The following day the plane took off normally. I had noticed this man again. This time he was being questioned by a purser on why he was sitting in an upper class seat with an economy ticket. I was unable to hear his reply but I noted that he remained seated. The flight was uneventful and soon we were getting ready to land.

"As I reread [the courier company's] instructions I saw, with great apprehension this man walking along the aisle. He was looking at each passenger and I knew, instinctively, that for some reason he was looking for me and I was right. He sat in the empty passenger seat next to me. Looking at me firmly he said 'I'll take all your manifests. I will be through customs before you.'

"Returning his firm look with what I hoped was one of my own, I said 'No, that's all right, thank you.'

"He gave me a look of surprise and hurt and said, 'You will be hanging about there all night. Give them to me. I know where to take them.'

"'That's quite alright, thank you. I have telephone numbers to ring should there be any problems.'

"'Look,' he said, 'You don't know when they will turn up. Where do you keep them? In your bag?'

"He nodded towards my holdall that I had placed on the other empty seat next to me. He was right; that is exactly where they were. My heart was pounding once more. I had no experience of this work and did not really know what to expect. Clearly though, I was responsible for these manifests and also for the cargo that they represented.

"'Look,' I said. 'I don't know who you are from Adam and I have no authority to give these documents to anyone.'

"'One minute,' he said and with that he left. He had obviously

75

gone for something which gave me time to compose myself and to work the next bit out. I made certain that the zip was firmly closed on my bag and then, dismissing the fleeting thought that perhaps I should go and sit somewhere else as the action of a coward, I made up my mind that he would not take these documents off me.

"He returned and showed me a card with his photograph and the name of a company on it which seemed hardly like a ticket to take the manifests. The discussion, which was getting a little heated on both sides, continued until shortly before the landing when he returned to his seat.

"As I walked away from the plane I saw him hanging around and he waited for me to come alongside of him. I ignored him and went to collect my suitcase.

"The cargo doors had jammed on the plane so there was a delay before I was able to leave. The first person I saw, on leaving customs, was the [courier company] representative. With a relieved smile I handed him the manifests.

"'You would have saved us all a lot of trouble if you had given these to Les when he asked you,' he spat at me.

"'What a fool I would have looked if you were asking me for these and I told you that I had given them to a complete stranger on the plane,' I said.

"'He was an employee of [the airline] for thirty years,' I was told.

"'But I didn't know that,' I said.

"'I know him very well,' said the rep. It seemed pointless arguing so I left.

"As a postnote, I did feel quite embarrassed over the incident but I have to say that I firmly believe, given the circumstances, that I acted correctly and until I am given detailed instructions that clearly specify that I am to part with these manifests to persons other than the courier representative I will act in exactly the same manner again. Much better a few people are upset than a consignment goes missing."

I agree completely and the courier company involved should have been pleased that (in the obvious absence of instructions from them to the contrary) this courier protected their paperwork so assiduously.

There are some other points about professionalism that are part of the fine print of the contracts you sign that you should be aware of.

You are expected to dress neatly and conservatively. Now Voyager specifies jacket and tie for men while IBC makes a jacket optional. For women, Now Voyager stipulates "dress, suit, or other businesslike attire," and draws the line at "faded" blue jeans for either gender. IBC says it tolerates jeans if they are "clean, pressed, and unfaded." However, they draw the line at "thongs, suggestive T-shirts, shorts, and unconventional hairstyles."

On my early flights, I always dressed like a businessman but I noticed that the dress regulations seemed to be honored more in the breach than the observance. On one trip, I found myself waiting at customs with a Brazilian student wearing a faded t-shirt and shorts and a young woman from Britain in tattered jeans. I suspect this happens because the courier company (which is usually represented by a fairly low-level employee) only gets to see what the courier is wearing a short time before the flight. It's probably easier to let it slide than to bar the courier from the flight and find a replacement.

I have now adopted a two-tier policy toward my courier wardrobe. If my activities at my destination will require a jacket and tie, I wear them on the flight. This not only meets the most stringent courier regulations but has the additional advantage of saving space in my carry-on luggage. Otherwise, I dress more casually but neatly and I have never had a problem.

Another common provision in most courier contracts prohibits consuming alcohol before or during your flight. "The Freelance Courier agrees to consume no alcohol in flight," says the Now Voyager contract in no uncertain language. SOS International Courier's contract stipulates only that you maintain "a strictly professional and sober manner during the flights and thereafter until all of Courier's duties hereunder are fully discharged," which would seem to imply that you could drink just so long as you remained (or, at least, acted) sober. Jupiter's contract makes no mention of alcohol.

Certainly no one has ever given me a breatholizer test when I arrived and I know other couriers who admit to imbibing en route. I suspect that the courier companies are most concerned about having a courier roll off a flight roaring drunk, thus complicating and delaying the customs process.

This suspicion was confirmed by a tale I was told recently of a woman who was serving as a courier on a Concorde flight from London to New York. The Concorde, among its many attractions, features an open bar. The lady in question proceeded to become quite drunk and rowdy, so much so that she had to be restrained by the attendants.

Unfortunately for the courier company that had put her on the plane, this Concorde flight was diverted from Kennedy to Newark. There are few situations in which the common sense of a courier can make a difference, but this was one of them. As it transpired, by the time the plane touched down at Newark, the courier in question was senseless and had to be wheeled off the flight — literally.

Fortunately for all concerned, she had been seated next to a courier for another company (who told this lurid tale) who explained the situation to the flight attendants and customs, was able to take charge of the situation, and looked after the now-abandoned courier shipment until the people who were picking it up made the long, inconvenient journey from JFK to Newark.

So be forewarned. If you do decide to indulge in flight, be discreet.

If you're like me, any discussion of contracts and legal responsibilities may leave you feeling slightly queasy. Lawyers are paid, a lawyer-friend once told me, to imagine all the horrible things that can possibly go wrong and then protect their clients against them.

The lawyers who draft these contracts for the courier companies are no exception. That is why courier contracts are liberally spiced with cheerful words like "loss or damage," "personal injuries," "cancellation," "accidents," and that all-time favorite, "death." They tend to be long on what the courier company can expect from you and short on what you can expect from the courier company.

In practice, courier travel is just as uneventful as "regular" travel. The worst-case scenarios envisioned by the courier contracts are unlikely to occur. And it might be noted that when you purchase a regular airline ticket you are agreeing to page after page of fine print (in effect, a "contract") which severely limits your rights and recourse against the airline.

Nonetheless, the fact remains that a contract is a contract and flying as a courier obligates you to play by rules that are different from those that apply to other forms of air travel. At a minimum, you should read the contracts carefully and make sure you understand and are comfortable with their provisions. If you have any questions or reservations, seek the advice of a competent professional.

To keep *my* lawyer happy, let me repeat that I am not of that noble profession and that nothing in this book should be construed as rendering legal advice.

Chapter Eight

The Avid Courier

For most people, courier travel is a sometime thing. It's a way to take an occasional holiday and nothing more. People like this may fly once every year or two. For others, courier travel becomes tantamount to a way of life. These are what I call "avid couriers."

The avid courier, in my experience, tends to fall into one of two broad categories: retirees and business travelers. For retired people, courier travel offers a perfect match — they have the time at their disposal, they can be completely flexible as to dates, and they are living, by and large, on a fixed income which makes the low cost of courier travel especially attractive.

George Sprague, a retired social worker for the county of San Diego, is a perfect example. He takes a minimum of three "vacations" a year and has visited Singapore, Bangkok, Tokyo, Seoul, Hong Kong, and Taipei as a courier. Most of the time he travels free by taking advantage of the need for last-minute couriers.

"If you book well in advance, you pay the advertised fare," he explains, "but I find out what flights they have going for a whole month. Then a day or two before the flight I call them up and ask, 'Is this flight open?' If it's open, fine, I'll take it because I know it's going to be free."

Obviously, it doesn't work every time and this is where a retiree's time flexibility comes into play. "I may have to make a dozen calls before I get a flight," George notes, but his track record proves that, with a little perseverance, a free flight will be forthcoming. "They've even called me on two occasions and said, 'We've got a flight going and it's free if you want it.' So they obviously have my name on their computer and they go down the list and say, 'This guy's gone a lot, let's try him.'"

Other retirees will pick a favorite destination and plan on going when they can get there super-cheap. According to Tom Belmont of Halbart's Miami office, "We have people who call up and say, 'Look, I have a granddaughter at school in England. If you ever have something going for $100 or less, give me a call.'"

For business travelers, even if they can easily afford full fare and are at the platinum level in all the frequent flyer programs, the lure of courier fares can be hard to pass up. A perfect example is Jonathon Steinberg, the international lawyer with offices in London and New York. He travels back and forth as a courier eight to twelve times each year.

There are a number of factors that make courier travel a natural for the businessperson. First and foremost is cost. I have business interests in Europe that might never have come about without the ability to get back and forth cheaply. Courier flights offer an ideal way of exploring new markets or checking out potential suppliers — and any money saved on airfare goes directly to the bottom line. And since most business travelers are flying by themselves, the solo nature of courier flights is no liability whatsoever.

In this Chapter I will discuss strategies and techniques you can use to join the ranks of avid couriers by establishing yourself as an asset for the various courier companies.

The first step in becoming an avid courier is to get to know the industry and the people in it. This will tend to happen naturally as you take one courier trip after another. However, you can and should take the initiative.

When you travel as an air courier through a booking agent, get to know the people you meet. While you are waiting for your flight, pass the time by asking the courier company rep a few "innocent" questions: What's the best way to deal directly with your company? Who should I ask for when I call? Where else do you fly to? Do you know any other companies I might call for courier flights? Can I get any special deals from your company if I can fly at the last minute?

You probably won't be able to ask every question you might have. You have to remember that, for the courier company, you are no more important — in fact, you're probably *less* important — than the paperwork that accompanies the shipment. Don't expect the reps to entertain you; they are not tour guides. I have discovered that the hallmark of the professional air courier is an air of calm self-assurance and asking too many "dumb" questions can blow the image.

Nonetheless, people are people and they tend to react positively to genuine interest in what they do. If you hit it off with a courier company rep, you can get some good, straight-from-the-shoulder information. And remember to *listen* to the answers you get.

Make a special note of any jargon that's specific to the courier business. The more you know about how the business in general and specific companies in particular work, the easier it will be to deal direct. On the other hand, don't expect everyone you meet to be an industry expert. As in any other business, some of the reps you meet will know how to do their specific job — and nothing else.

Another good source of information is the person who meets you at customs on your return. This person may not represent a courier company at all. In New York, it's often a representative of New York Air Courier Clearance (NYACC). At London's Heathrow, it may be someone from Courier Facilities Ltd. These are not courier companies but clearing houses which handle the customs hassle for a number of different companies. Consequently, they can give you the latest information on who's still in business and where they fly to.

Yet another source of valuable information is your fellow couriers. Often you will find yourself hanging out at customs with one or two other couriers. Ask them who they're flying for and quiz them for tips on other companies they have flown for. Get their home addresses and keep in touch. Let them know that you would appreciate it if they could pass along any new information they might pick up on their travels.

For example, I am indebted to fellow courier Warren Halliday, who tipped me off to World Courier's new service to Mexico City. Other couriers have alerted me to new contacts, not just in far-flung cities, but right here in my home base of New York.

W hile you want to get to know the courier companies, your ultimate goal is to have them get to know you. "The secret of courier travel is to build up a relationship with these companies and show them that you're reliable," advises courier lawyer Jonathon Steinberg. "So that whenever there's a choice between using you or using someone else, you'll hope they'll always want to use you."

There's a theory that if you make casual contact with anyone three times, they will remember who you are. Put this theory to work as you set out to establish yourself as a reliable courier.

Make a note, mental or otherwise, of the names of all your contacts in the air courier business. This is a basic networking technique. Your goal is to get them to remember you as a reliable and professional courier. Being able to ask for the right person when you call or ask, "How's Jimmy doing?" gives you a leg up.

Another way to establish an identity with a courier company is to send a short thank-you note after each trip. Often, the instruction sheets and other materials you are given when you travel as a courier will alert you to the appropriate person to whom to address your note. Sending these "bread-and-butter" notes is another well-established business practice that will be familiar to anyone who has been in sales or marketing. Here are some suggestions for making your notes most effective:

- Send your note to the head of the company if possible.
- Make a point to commend any of their employees who have been particularly friendly or helpful.
- You also might to want to drop subtle hints about how often you fly: "This was my fifth courier trip with you. "
- Type your note on business stationery if you have it. Otherwise, hand-write it neatly on personalized stationery.
- If you know you will be available to fly at a certain time in the future or go at short notice, offer your services.

85

Steinberg suggests another way to win share of mind with the courier companies. "When I'm going across the Atlantic and a client is paying, I'll often call up [a courier company] and say 'Do you need a courier for tomorrow? I'm going over.'" He is, in effect, offering his services at no charge to the courier company and at no additional inconvenience to him. If the company has had a last-minute cancellation, an offer like this can be a life-saver. It's also possible that the company might find it useful to use Steinberg's ticket to ship some additional cargo. Even if the courier company can't take him up on the offer (which is the most likely scenario), he has further established himself as an asset to the company.

It should be pointed out that an offer like this will be much more meaningful coming from someone the company knows well — like Steinberg — than from a stranger off the street. You may want to hold off using this ploy until you have established a track record with the company.

A bove and beyond all else, the would-be avid courier must establish a reputation for complete and utter professionalism and reliability.

"Look at it from their point of view," says Steinberg, referring to the courier companies. "They're in a quandary. They've got to put people on planes. They've got to make sure those people are reliable. But they've got to put so many people on planes so often that there's no way they can ascertain whether all these people really are reliable. So what you have to do is show these people that you're someone they can do business with.

"And that's the important point," he stresses. "They've got to know who they can rely on. These guys have been stung a lot. People have a tendency, even when they've paid a couple of hundred dollars for the ticket and might lose it, not to show up for the flight. When someone doesn't show up for the flight they've got to send their station manager out to England. Then they're without their station manager for two days and it costs them a fortune."

When you hear a few stories like that you begin to understand why courier companies are constantly hoping that some day they'll be able to find a way to avoid using on-boards at all. All the more reason to make a special effort to be on time and follow instructions to the letter. Dress neatly and don't roll off the plane blind drunk. By conducting yourself in a professional manner at all times, you are not only helping establish your own reputation but you are doing a favor for all freelance on-board couriers.

T he Holy Grail of the avid courier is the free flight. They are available. They are not available every day of the week but they crop up with surprising regularity. In my case, because I monitor flight availability so regularly, I have found that it's not the free flights that are so rare but the free flights that coincide with my schedule!

Many air courier companies have established procedures for handling last-minute openings. I have given complete details (when available) in the "International Air Courier Directory."

Here is a strategy to use regardless of whether the courier company has published guidelines for last-minute openings. It works best if you have already established a track record as a reliable courier but I know of first-time couriers who have used it successfully. It requires that you be ready to go at a moment's notice (i.e., you have a bag already packed) and be willing to go to any destination to which the courier company travels.

Give all the courier companies in your preferred departure cities a call and briefly explain your situation. "I'm available to travel to any of your destinations from Monday the fourth to Sunday the tenth. Call me if you get a cancellation. Of course, since I'm willing to go anywhere on such short notice, I'll expect your absolute lowest fare."

If the company has established last-minute fares, they may not be subject to negotiation. Otherwise, you should feel free to negotiate for the lowest fare when you first call or, if you have the gall, when they call you and you know they're desperate. Be careful, however. The courier companies provide you with a very good deal. Taking advantage of them when they're in a bind can backfire. After all, it's a small world.

Another possible ploy is to call with basically the same proposition except that this time you say, "I'm only willing to go if you can waive the fare. So call me only if you're really desperate. I guarantee that I will be able to leave for the airport as soon as you call me."

Either approach presupposes that you will be able to deliver on your promise. If they call and you say, "Oh, gee, well my plans changed and I can't make it," you can forget ever dealing with that company again. It follows that if you book a flight with one company using this strategy, you *immediately* call any others you have contacted and inform them that you have booked a flight and are no longer available.

Don't overlook timing when laying your plans to grab a free or ultra-low cost fare. "During the summer months, getting a free flight is almost impossible," says George Sprague, speaking of the Far Eastern destinations that are his favorites. "All the college kids are out of school and they're willing to pay the regular fare. But if you go in November, December, January, or February — which is the best time of year to go to places like Singapore and Bangkok — you can almost always get a free flight."

And don't forget other factors that might create a window of opportunity for the die-hard bargain hunter. As I noted earlier, both the Gulf War and the eruption of Mount Pinatubo spawned a rash of low-cost courier flights for those brave enough to go against conventional wisdom.

At the far end of the spectrum, of course, are those couriers who are available all the time to go anywhere. If you have established yourself with a courier company as someone who *regularly* takes advantage of last minute flights then it may not be so important that you are not available on one particular occasion. The courier company will simply go on to the next call and keep you on their list.

Remember that there is competition for these low- or no-cost opportunities. Some companies have told me that they have long lists of people who say they are available at short notice. Your challenge is to give yourself every possible advantage.

Even though the courier company may have a "take a number and wait in line" system — or claim they do — a simple understanding of human nature tells us that other factors come into play. For one thing, human beings play favorites which is why it is so important to establish your profile as a reliable courier. When a slot opens up, you want them to think of you first.

I also suspect that you can better your chances by making it easier for the company to remember you and contact you. For example, if you are telling a company that you are available to travel during the coming week you might want to fax them a sort of advertisement for your availability which they can stick up on their bulletin board. That way if something comes up, your eye-catching notice may give you an advantage. If you are constantly looking for available flights, consider providing the companies in your area of interest with tabbed rolodex cards that say something like "Emergency Courier," or "Last-Minute Courier to England."

T he final frontier for the avid courier is finding a way of flying as a courier with companies that will swear up and down that they never use freelance on-board couriers.

"If a company claims it's not using an on-board courier," says Steinberg, "then it cannot be in control of how quickly its packages get across the Atlantic because its packages must be going with the airline as air freight when the airline next sends out a freight plane. Now they're not in control of how long the things stays in the airline's warehouse before it gets loaded onto the plane or when the plane is going because there's no such thing as a scheduled air freight service, really. And they're not in control of off-loading the stuff when it gets to wherever it's going. I'd always be very suspicious if people say we don't use on-board couriers anymore."

The fact of the matter is that even the industry heavyweights with their own fleets of planes sometimes have a need for a human being to actually accompany a shipment on a regular airline. The question becomes where do they get them? In some cases, they actually can call on their own people. DHL, for example, has regular runs to the Caribbean which they make available at no cost to their own vacationing employees. Because they are such a large company, they apparently can fill the available slots. When they can't, they turn to a booking agent to plug the holes. It is also possible that a company that normally co-loads with a wholesaler might find itself in a situation to temporarily use its own on-board courier.

Sometimes, unusual circumstances can create a need for an on-board courier. "If someone like Salomon Brothers is putting in a bid for a $5 billion company in Europe," muses Steinberg, "and they want someone to hand-carry that bid across, they may contact the courier company they are using at the moment and say 'We've got a special, private, rush job. We want this thing taken over immediately, hand-carried, and hand-delivered. Do you have someone who can do it?'

"Well, the courier company obviously won't have anyone [on staff] that they can use to do it but they will have a list of people who are reliable who they can use. But the trouble is, it's going to be quite difficult to get on that list, isn't it?"

The "courier curtain" can be difficult, if not impossible, to penetrate. Courier companies, for very good reasons, don't like to discuss their methods of operation with strangers making inquiries on the phone. In any event, it's an assignment only for the die-hard courier who is willing and able to travel at the last-minute to anywhere, since that's virtually the only situation in which an opportunity might develop.

If you'd like to try it anyway and you live in or near one of the gateway cities, begin by compiling a list of local courier companies from the phone book. You may be able to eliminate some as being inappropriate, but in this case it's probably better to canvas them all. Then follow the suggestions given above for last-minute, go-anywhere couriers. Don't bother to phone. Just send a letter to the "Director of Courier Operations" (a good catch-all title) explaining that you are available to travel on short notice as an on-board courier should the need arise. Let them know you are an experienced courier by citing the companies you have flown for and giving references if possible. Then sit back, cross your fingers, and wait for the phone to ring.

Oh yes, one more thing. Don't hold your breath.

Part II

International
Air Courier
Directory

Introduction to the Directory

In the following chapters I provide listings of courier companies and booking agencies throughout the world. The arrangement is somewhat idiosyncratic, as follows:

Canada: Listed alphabetically by city, then by company name.

United States: Here the arrangement is geographical, starting with the East coast and moving westward — New York, Miami, Chicago, Houston, San Francisco and Los Angeles. This way, it seemed to me, the cities that are closest to you would be closest to each other in the listings.

England: Since most of the courier companies in England are clustered to the West of London, around Heathrow airport, I have arranged them alphabetically by company name.

Other Overseas Contacts: Listed alphabetically by country, then by company name.

Destination Index: This index allows you to link cities with the air courier companies that serve them.

Additional explanatory notes and comments appear at the beginning of each chapter. It may not be the most elegant arrangement but it strikes me as serviceable.

Most of the companies listed are actively dealing with freelance, on-board couriers. However, I have included a number of companies that used to use freelancers but have discontinued the practice. That's because policies change in the air courier business — sometimes overnight. If you're desperate, or merely curious, they might be worth a call, just in case.

For each contact listed I have tried to give a fairly comprehensive overview of their current situation — where they fly, how much they charge, and what their policies and procedures are. Don't assume, however, that the entries are encyclopedic. In other words, just because a listing of courier company "x" makes no mention of last-minute reduced fares, doesn't automatically imply that they are never offered.

Remember: companies go out of business and new ones spring up to take their place. Freight companies that use freelance couriers today, may change their policy tomorrow. You will always have to double-check to see what the current policy is and what flights are available. The same applies in reverse. Companies not listed here, may begin to seek freelancers. Check the Yellow Pages of the major air courier origination points for new possibilities. (You can find them in any large public library). If you do succeed in uncovering a new source of courier bookings, please let me know. See the special offer at the back of this book.

Unless otherwise noted, flights leave from the city listed. Getting to the point of departure is always the courier's responsibility.

CANADA

The Canadian market for courier travel is, alas, shrinking. TNT Express Worldwide is no longer using freelancers for its flights out of Canada, having switched to British Airways' Speedbird service. But perhaps the greatest loss was the cancellation of F. B.'s Toronto to Miami run, a real bargain for Canadian sun-worshippers. Still, there are good bargains to be had to desirable destinations.

By the way, all fares listed from Canadian cities are quoted in *Canadian* dollars, which trade at about a 10% - 14% discount to the American dollar. Factor that in when doing your budgeting.

[Note: to dial direct to Canada from the United Kingdom, first dial (010) which tells the phone company you are making an international call. Then dial (1), which is Canada's "country code." Then dial the numbers listed below. From the United States, of course, a call to Canada is like any other long-distance call.]

MONTREAL

F.B. On-Board Courier Service
10105 Ryan Avenue
Dorval, Quebec H9P 1A2
(514) 633-0740 to book flights
(514) 631-7925, administrative offices
At present F.B.'s Montreal operation flies only to London, although they tell me they may be offering a run to Paris in the future.

There are five flights each week to London with stays of either eight, ten, or twelve days depending on your day of departure. Round trip fares are their highest at Christmas time ($450) and can drop as low as $300 when F. B. can get special pricing from the airlines.

You must carry a passport that allows you to enter England without a visa. Payment is by cash, cashier's check, or money order. There is no return guarantee deposit.

Jet Services
2735 Paulus Street
Ville St. Laurent
Montreal, Quebec H4S 1E9
(800) 361-4969
(514) 331-7470
(514) 331-3451 (Fax)
This small operation has five flights a week to Paris, their only destination, Mondays through Friday. The round-trip fare doesn't vary seasonally and has been holding steady at $350 for the last year or so but may go up in the near future.

The length of stay varies with the day of departure. On Monday flights, you can stay 13 days. Tuesday and Wednesday departures are for a one week stay. Thursday and Friday departures have a two week turnaround.

Jet Services requires couriers to be at least 18; they have an upper age cut off of 65. There is no return-guarantee deposit required and you can get frequent flyer mileage credit on the Air France and Air Canada flights they use. On the debit side, they tell me they never offer reduced, last-minute fares.

You can generally book flights up to six weeks or more in advance and must make booking arrangements in person; you will also be required to pay for your ticket in full at that time. Payment must be in cash, cashier's check, or via a Canadian or US dollars money order. The best time to call for information about flight availability is between 11:00 and 1:00 EST. Ask to speak with John Rustom.

TORONTO

F.B. On-Board Courier Service
83 Galaxy Boulevard, Unit 34
Rexdale, Ontario M9W 5X6
(416) 675-1820
(514) 633-0740 to book flights
F.B. has flights to both London and Hong Kong out of Toronto but you must make all arrangements through their Montreal office, where they have centralized their booking.

London fares are the same as those listed for Montreal, above, although their are six flights each week from Toronto. The stays are eight, ten, or twelve days depending on the day of the week you leave.

Fares to Hong Kong were recently quoted as $1,000 during the winter and $1,200 in the summer. There are five flights each week. These flights make a stop in Vancouver (see below), but you cannot board as a courier from there.

VANCOUVER

F.B. On-Board Courier Service
5200 Miller Road, Suite 116
Richmond, British Columbia V7B 1X8
(604) 278-1266
F. B.'s Vancouver operation offers five flights each week to London. Recently, round trip fares were being quoted at $425 during the low season and $525 during high season. The length of stay depends on your day of departure, as follows: Monday, Thursday, and Saturday departures are for ten days; Tuesday and Wednesday departures are for 15 days. It's an extremely popular run which is usually booked up six to seven months in advance. Flights are via Air Canada and offer frequent flyer points.

Unlike the Toronto office, the Vancouver office handles its own bookings. Ask for Jim or Dee Marshall when you call. Payment may be made in cash or personal check (no credit cards).

Jim maintains a stand-by list for last-minute cancellations but don't get too excited. "There are approximately 25 to 30 people on the stand-by list at any one time," he says, "and we only get two or three cancellations a year."

They also handle courier runs between Vancouver and Hong Kong but at the present time all couriers on these flights originate out of Hong Kong. See the listing for the Hong Kong office of Line Haul Express in "Other Overseas Contacts," below, in case you ever find yourself stranded in Hong Kong.

UNITED STATES

This chapter is arranged geographically, from east to west. That is, you will find courier gateway cities listed in the following order: New York, Miami, Chicago, Houston, San Francisco, and Los Angeles.

If a company has offices in more than one city, I have given the most complete information about policies and procedures under the office in the "headquarters" city.

[Note: to dial direct to the United States from the United Kingdom, first dial (010) which tells the phone company you are making an international call. Then dial (1), which is the United States' "country code." Then dial the numbers listed below. From Canada, of course, a call to the United States is like any other long-distance call.]

NEW YORK

N ew York is without a doubt the air courier capital of the United States. No other gateway city comes close, either in terms of the number of companies booking on-board couriers or the number of destinations served.

There are now three major booking agencies in the New York area: Courier Travel Service, Discount Travel International, and Now Voyager. They offer pretty much the same flights (with some minor differences) and pretty much the same fares. Their major differentiator is the level and quality of service they provide and you, the consumer, will have to be the judge of that.

That's not to say that excellent opportunities can't be found elsewhere — through other, smaller, operations or directly with air freight wholesalers and retailers. They can. The following listings give the details.

Able Travel & Tours
18 East 41st Street
New York, NY 10017
(212) 779-8530
The people at Able describe themselves as "a unique full-service travel agency" in that they offer courier flights to London and Paris as well as discounted, consolidator tickets to all major destinations in Western Europe. They are currently considering expanding their courier offerings to other destinations as well.

At press time, round-trip fares were being quoted at $295 to London and $345 to Paris. Generally, Able likes to undercut the courier fares offered by other booking agencies by a few dollars. Knowing what the others are currently offering will help you get the best fare. Able does not keep any list of last-minute couriers and offers no last-minute specials.

Able will also let you book as far in advance as you want with the understanding that they may not always be able to get immediate confirmation from the cargo company. This service allows you to plan well in advance if you know you definitely want to be in London or Paris on a specific date.

Payment is by cash, money order, or personal check (no credit cards) and must be made as soon as possible after booking your flight. Otherwise, you run the risk of losing the booking. If you are booking from out of town, plan on using overnight mail or Federal Express.

One- and two-week stays are available, although they may not always be able to accommodate you. Flights are available any day of the week except Sunday. Check to see if they can book you and a companion on the same day (different flights) or on succeeding days. No return-guarantee deposit is required. Going for frequent flyer credit is your responsibility; do it at the airport.

When you call to book, ask for Ed. They may try to steer you away from courier travel, citing the air freight company's right to bump you from the flight if a company employee needs to make the trip. This is, indeed, a risk of courier travel but a minor one.

Able is also a consolidator and a good source of short-notice, non-courier bargains. They will "back-date" domestic and international tickets, thus allowing you to avoid advance purchase requirements. If your European travel will start and end some distance from New York, you may want to check with Able to see if they can offer a competitive direct ticket. In other words, it may be that a ticket purchased from Able from Denver, say, to London and back might cost about as much as (or even less than) the combined cost of a Denver-New York-Denver ticket and a New York-London-New York courier flight. Of course, you might want to check with other consolidators as well.

Air Facility
153-40 Rockaway Boulevard
Jamaica, NY 11434
(718) 712-0630
(718) 712-1574 (Fax)
Air Facility is an air courier wholesaler serving South America. Recently, they were serving the following destinations:

Destination (Airline)	Departure Days	Length of Stay	Typical Fare
Buenos Aires (Varig)	Tuesday Wednesday Thursday	10 days 12 days 12 days	$530
Buenos Aires (Lan Chile)	Monday Wednesday Thursday Saturday	6 days 13 days 8 days 12 days	$480
Caracas (Pan Am, Avensa)	Sunday Monday Tuesday Wednesday Thursday	6 days 8 days 9 days 7 days 8 days	$210
Montevideo (Varig)	Tuesday Wednesday Thursday	10 days 12 days 12 days	$570
Rio (Varig)	Monday Tuesday Saturday	10 days 15 days 9 days	$480 $580 $480
Santiago (Lan Chile)	Tuesday	13 days	$480

Air Facility requires that its couriers be at least 21 years of age; there is no upper age cut off. You must be either a citizen of the U.S. or have resident alien status ("green card"). Non-residents who are in the U.S. on tourist visas are not eligible to fly with Air Facility.

They prefer it if you book at least one month in advance and then pay as soon as possible by cash, certified check, or money order; no credit cards or personal checks are accepted. You can cancel your reservation and get a refund up to 15 days before the flight.

If you are available to fly at short notice, call and let them know the dates you are available and the destination(s) you are willing to accept. If they get a cancellation, they will give you a call. Ask for Ruth.

Airhitch
2790 Broadway, Suite 100
New York, NY 10025
(212) 864-2000
Airhitch is not an air courier company, but a student-run organization specializing in space-available travel to Europe at steep discounts comparable to those available to couriers. Here's how it works:

Register with Airhitch, giving them the earliest, latest, and preferred dates of departure, and three choices of destination in Europe. You are instructed to call back as your "date-range" approaches; they will tell you what's available. You must accept one of the flights offered — even if it's not to your primary destination — or forfeit your fare. Like air courier operations, Airhitch is designed for the independent traveler for whom a change in destination will be an adventure rather than a disaster.

Airhitch lists its "primary" destinations as Amsterdam, Brussels, Frankfort, Geneva, London, Madrid, Milan, Munich, Paris, Rome, Stuttgart, and Zurich. Current **one-way** fares are $160 from New York, $269 from the West coast, and $229 from "anywhere else" (the Midwest, Denver, Texas, or the Southeast). Return trips are booked separately, either before departure or through an Airhitch associate in Europe.

Airhitch claims that 90% of their travelers flew directly to one of their preferred destinations or to a city within "commuting distance," and that 100% of registrants "who followed our guidelines" flew during their "date-range." The Airhitch system favors those who register far in advance of their desired travel dates, as the date of registration determines the order in which people are offered available seats. It also helps if you can spend an extended amount of time in Europe.

Occasional special, low-cost flights are offered when Airhitch finds a carrier or charter operator with a large number of seats to unload at short notice. For example, New York to Germany flights were once available for $139 one-way. On another occasion, Airhitch was able to provide confirmed seats to Paris for $160, one-way. You must be registered and fully paid-up at the regular fare to be eligible for these bargains, however.

For those who don't live in or near the major jumping-off points for couriers, Airhitch's best feature may be the range of departure cities it offers. European flights have been available (on an irregular basis) from Seattle, Denver, Minneapolis, Detroit, Tampa, Fort Lauderdale, Baltimore, and Cleveland.

Airhitch has a brochure with detailed information on their policies and procedures. The New York office is open 10 a.m. to 5 p.m. EST. After hours, a voice mail system — the "Airhitch Robot" — provides extensive information about their offerings. There is also a Los Angeles office.

Brinks Air Courier
1 Battery Park Plaza
New York, NY 10004
(212) 558-6267
No freelancers. Uses its own highly trained and bonded specialists to transport extremely valuable cargo such as diamonds. I

have listed them here specifically because Brink's is an excellent career choice if you want a job that includes international travel.

Canadex
Building 89, JFK Airport
Jamaica, NY 11430
(718) 917-0710
(718) 917-0718 (Fax)

Canadex flies its own fleet of cargo planes into Canada but doesn't use couriers on those runs. From time to time, Canadex will institute on-board courier runs to other destinations when it "sees a void in the marketplace." In recent years, that has meant runs to Mexico City and Venezuela, although, at press time, they had no such "outside runs" operating. When they do add such routes to their schedule, they do all their booking of on-board couriers through Now Voyager and Courier Travel Service (see below).

Courier Network
295 7th Avenue
New York, NY 10001
(212) 691-9860
(212) 675-6876
(212) 929-5186 (Fax)

Flies to Tel Aviv six days a week and uses freelancers. It's obviously a very popular route. A recent enquiry turned up a cancellation in nine weeks; the next regularly scheduled flight available was more than three months away. Stays in Israel can range from one week to two months. The flight out to Israel takes a day and a half, the return trip, one day. Keep that in mind when planning your length of stay. "Most people go for at least two weeks," they tell me. Another attraction is that you will be allowed one checked piece of luggage in addition to your carry-on allotment. The round-trip fare varies from $520 to $650 depending on the time of year.

Many of Courier Network's couriers plan their vacations in Israel, I am told. Consequently, they say, there is little call for last-minute couriers. Nonetheless, they will take your name, just in case, if you are free to travel on short notice.

To enquire about flight availability and to book your trip, call between 7 p.m. and 9 p.m. EST. Ask for Alazar.

Courier Travel Service
530 Central Avenue
Cedarhurst, NY 11516
(516) 374-2299
(800) ASK-2FLY
(800) 922-2FLY
(516) 374-2261 (Fax)

Courier Travel Service is a booking agent which, under the direction of Marvin Singer, is seeking to become *the* major player in the field. As such, they are in head-to-head competition with Discount Travel International and Now Voyager (see below). They charge no annual "membership" fee and Marvin tells me they have no plans to do so. You will have to weigh that advantage against the fact that, by and large, their fares are somewhat higher than those offered through Now Voyager; a recent comparison of fares showed Now Voyager to be more expensive on two routes, the same on four, and less expensive on six others. When you are ready to fly, a little comparison shopping will tell you where your best deal lies.

From New York, Courier Travel offers broad coverage of Europe, as well as offering flights to Israel, South America, and the Orient. According to Marvin, they book for "ten to twelve" different air freight companies. Recently, the following European destinations were available:

Destination (Airline)	Departure Days	Length of Stay	Fare Range
Amsterdam (KLM)	Monday to Thursday & Saturday	One week	$329 - $399
Brussels (Sabena)	Monday to Thursday & Saturday	One week	$299 - $379
Copenhagen (KLM)	Monday to Thursday & Saturday	One week	$299 - $379
Frankfort (Lufthansa)	Monday to Thursday & Saturday	One week	$329 - $399
London (American)	Monday to Thursday & Saturday	Up to 30 days	$299 - $349
London (American)	Monday to Saturday	One week	$249 - $329
Madrid (Iberia)	Monday to Saturday	One week (Sat. deps. 9 days)	$349 - $429
Milan (Alitalia)	Monday to Thursday & Saturday	Two weeks (Sat. & Mon. deps. 11 days)	$399 - $449
Paris (TWA)	Monday to Thursday & Saturday	One week	$349 - $429
Rome (Alitalia)	Monday to Thursday & Saturday	8 days (Sat. deps. ret. from Milan, 9 days)	$399 - $429

Destination (Airline)	Departure Days	Length of Stay	Fare Range
Stockholm (Finnair)	Tuesday to Thursday & Saturday	One week	$299 - $379
Zurich (American)	Monday to Thursday & Saturday	One week	$349 - $429

Even its competitors will admit that Courier Travel Service "controls the book" to London. One of the best deals at CTS is their London option with stays of up to 30 days. I've taken advantage of this when I've wanted to be in London on specific dates and for specific lengths of time. As long as you're booking far enough in advance, CTS will even let you change your dates to lengthen or shorten your stay. Also, with 26 flights *each week*, London is "pretty much available" whenever you call. The 30-day stay feature opens up a wealth of opportunities with their London contacts. Before you leave New York, you can make arrangements to fly on from London to other European destinations (that might not be available direct) or to exotic African destinations like Nairobi, Harare, and Johannesburg. No direct flights to Africa are available from New York.

CTS also offers flights to Hong Kong five days a week (Tuesday through Saturday) with flexible stays of from six to 30 days. The outbound trip is via JAL, with the return on Northwest. Recently, the round-trip fare was quoted at $599.

Also on the menu is a run to Tel Aviv. Departures are on TWA Monday through Saturday. Again, the stay is flexible from six to 30 days. The relatively high round-trip fare of $699 reflects the high demand on this route. TWA's lowest economy excursion fares range from $832 to $956, depending on the season.

110

Courier Travel Service also offers five destinations in South America from New York.

Destination (Airline)	Departure Days	Length of Stay	Typical Fare
Buenos Aires (Varig)	Call	9 to 10 days	$529
Buenos Aires (Lan Chile)	Monday	6 days	$529
	Tuesday	15 days	$629
	Wednesday	13 days	$529
	Thursday	8 days	$529
	Saturday	12 days	$529
Caracas (Avensa)	Daily	6 to 9 days	$249
Montevideo (Varig)	Wednesday	12 days	$699
Rio (Varig)	Saturday	9 days	$529
Santiago (Varig)	Tuesday	13 days	$529

Policies and Procedures

To fly as a courier through CTS you must be at least 18 years old and have a valid passport. There are no other qualifications and there is no upper age limit. In fact, Courier Travel Service has a warm spot in its heart for seniors. "They're very reliable," says owner Marvin Singer, "When they say they'll be there, they'll be there." Besides, "I'm a senior citizen myself," he notes. Senior citizens may be eligible for ten percent discounts on some flights, especially connecting flights from London to other European destinations.

Depending on the policies of the air freight company for which you will be serving as a courier, a $100 "return-guarantee"

111

deposit may be required. One courier told me that when flying through CTS he was told to be prepared to pay the departure tax and a $100 return-guarantee to the representative who would meet him at the airport and give him his ticket, but the rep never asked so the courier wound up saving a few extra dollars.

CTS has recently added an "automated attendant" to its telephone system. After hours you can call the (516) number and listen to Marvin telling you about "our exciting last-minute specials" (Press "2"). At press time, they were featuring a spate of $149 and $199 fares to European destinations. By pressing "1," you can hear a list of CTS's currently available world-wide destinations.

They recommend that you book six weeks to two months in advance although seats are also available on shorter notice. Ask them about the possibility of arranging cheap connecting flights from your home city or possible connections from your courier destination. Frequent flyer credit is available on some of the courier flights as well as on any connecting flights you may book. Once you have been ticketed on your courier flight, call the airline and put in your frequent flyer number.

Once you book your flight you must pay by cash, certified check, or money order only. You can make arrangements to pay for your tickets in Manhattan. Ask for Penny.

To book a flight, simply call the (516) number listed above and ask for Marvin or Cathy. Office hours are from 9:30 a.m. to 5 p.m. EST, Monday through Friday. It's best to have at least a general idea of where you want to go and when. They will tell you what's available. If you are interested in a multi-leg journey through London, ask for Marvin; he will help you hash out your itinerary on this call. My experience has been that they will really try to help you out if you are window shopping for destinations and dates. Just make sure you don't abuse their good will.

Courier Travel also offers occasional last-minute bargains if they have unfilled seats or cancellations. Call at 11 a.m. for flights that leave that night. Cut rate fares on these flights can range from $100 to $199 depending on the time of year. Remember: you will have to leave on extremely short notice, so be prepared!

They also can book you onto European flights leaving from Miami (see below) and may be able to get you on some courier flights from Los Angeles. Regardless of the departure city, all bookings are done through the New York office. At one time, CTS also offered flights from Toronto, Chicago, and Houston; they may again.

A new feature of CTS is what they call "our low fares to anywhere in the world from anywhere in the world." Just tell them your originating city, your destination city, and the approximate time of travel and they will quote you a fare.

Discount Travel International (DTI)
152 West 72nd Street
New York, NY 10023
(212) 362-8113
(212) 362-5310 (Fax, call first)
The very personable Dawn McCaffrey operates this new booking agency offering courier flights and other low-cost travel alternatives. The arrival of DTI means there are now three major booking agencies in the New York City area, all offering a similar list of destinations.

Destination (Airline)	Departure Days	Length of Stay	Typical Fare
Amsterdam (KLM)	Monday to Friday	One week	$250
Brussels (Sabena)	Monday to Saturday	One week	$299

Destination (Airline)	Departure Days	Length of Stay	Typical Fare
Copenhagen (KLM)	Monday to Thursday & Saturday	One week	$299
Frankfort (Lufthansa)	Monday to Saturday	One week	$299
London (American)	Monday to Saturday	One week	$250
Madrid (Iberia)	Monday to Saturday	One week	$299
Milan (Alitalia)	Monday to Saturday	Two weeks	$399
Paris (TWA)	Monday to Saturday	One week	$350
Rome (Alitalia)	Monday to Saturday	One week	$399
Stockholm (Finnair)	Monday to Saturday	One week	$299
Zurich (American)	Monday to Saturday	One week	$299

The following South American destinations are also offered:

Destination (Airline)	Departure Days	Length of Stay	Typical Fare
Buenos Aires (Lan Chile)	Monday Wednesday Thursday Saturday	9 days 13 days 8 days 12 days	$530
Caracas (Avensa)	Sunday Monday Tuesday Wednesday Thursday	6 days 8 days 9 days 7 days 8 days	$260

Destination (Airline)	Departure Days	Length of Stay	Typical Fare
Montevideo (Varig)	Wednesday	13 days	$650
Rio (Varig)	Monday Tuesday Saturday	10 days 15 days 9 days	$530
Santiago (Varig)	Tuesday	Call	$530
Mexico City (Aeromexico)	Monday to Saturday	Open return	$250

DTI also offers five flights each week to Hong Kong (Tuesday to Saturday), with stays of up to a month. Recently, the round-trip fare was quoted at $650.

Policies and Procedures

DTI requires no registration fee and prides itself on its high level of service and commitment to the discount traveler. They tell me they will make a special effort to accommodate those traveling together — by putting you both on the same plane as couriers for different companies, by booking you as couriers on different flights on the same or subsequent days, or by booking one as a courier and the other as a regular passenger on the same flight. Reservations can be made on the phone. Payment in full must be made in cash or by check or money order as soon as possible to hold the seat. Call between 10 a.m. and 5:30 p.m., Monday to Friday. After hours, a recorded announcement carries information on flight availability and fares.

Like any booking agency, DTI sometimes finds couriers for courier companies who are desperate to fill a seat. Most companies will try to make at least some money on these flights, but owner McCaffrey claims to see these situations as a marketing opportunity. "I've given away lots of free flights," she says, referring to these last-minute vacancies. "The courier company doesn't charge me anything, and I don't make any money on the deal, but these people will remember us and tell their friends about us and come back to use us again."

In addition to courier flights, DTI offers discounts on charter flights and even special fares from the airlines. For example, they have offered Christmas-time flights to Manchester, England, from Boston or New York for $511 round-trip; just before and just after the Christmas rush, these flights were pegged at $375 round-trip. Flights to London from several East Coast cities were also available for about the same amount.

In the past, DTI has offered courier flights to various of the Caribbean islands. Dawn tells me that these runs seem to be a thing of the past. The flights continue but the courier companies are giving the courier seats to their own employees as a perk. To fill this void, she is looking into providing charter flights to the area but has yet to seal a deal that will allow her to offer a sufficiently low fare. Check in for an update.

East-West Express
507-535 Rockaway Avenue
Valley Stream, NY 11581
or
P.O. Box 30849
JFK Station
Jamaica, NY 11430
(516) 561-2360
(516) 568-0477, Fax
East-West is now using freelance couriers for a run to Manila, only. They have discontinued their flights to Seoul, Korea, and Sydney, Australia, for the time being due to "lack of interest." "We could get more couriers to go to Manila than we could to

Seoul," they explained. "So we changed our destination." Cargo for those other destinations is now dropped off in Tokyo, to be forwarded, while the courier continues on to Manila.

"Things change so often in this business that you never know," they said, so these runs may be resurrected. Or new ones may come into being.

There are four flights each week to Manila, via Northwest Airlines. The fare is a relatively stiff $700. "That's high for couriers," they admit, "but we found we can get it." On the plus side, you can get frequent flyer miles and there is no return-guarantee deposit required. Stays are for two weeks. Sometimes, they can be flexible on the stays — "Let's say you wanted to go for one week and somebody wanted to go for three weeks, then it would work out." Generally, however, count on a two-week stay.

The flights book up fast, in spite of the high fare. That's because East-West's Manila service has proved popular with the large and growing Filipino population in the New York area, who are eager to take advantage of a cheap trip home. East-West tells me that their service is widely publicized in the Filipino community and that they use a Filipino booking agent (whose identity they didn't want to share).

Others can still call East-West directly. You should call at le*ast* two months in advance. Don't be surprised if they are booked solid for four or five months. Ask for Graham or Kristin. Once you have booked, payment must be made, in person, at their Valley Stream office. Cash is preferred.

If you can travel on short notice, East-West will put you on a list and call you if they have a cancellation. The fare in these cases is lower but not exceptional. "We've gone down to $400," they told me. "And if we're really desperate, we'll go even lower but we're usually not that desperate for Manila."

East-West used to maintain offices in San Francisco and Los Angeles, both of which are now closed.

Halbart Express
147-05 176th Street
Jamaica, NY 11434
(718) 656-8279
(718) 656-8189
(718) 244-0559 (Fax)

Halbart Express serves destinations in Western Europe only. According to owner Rudy Halbart, they are the largest courier operation in the New York area. "We send out 25 couriers each night," he says proudly. That adds up to approximately 150 each week.

Halbart is strictly a wholesaler. That is, they ship cargo for other companies which ship it for customers like you and me. Some of the major courier companies such as DHL, Federal Express, Burlington, and others are Halbart customers.

While they use several booking agents to find couriers for them, you can also book flights directly. You can reserve flights over the phone; Halbart will then send you a contract, which you must sign and return with full payment. Only then is your flight secured. Payment may be by cash, personal check, or money order; no credit cards are accepted. Expect to put up a return-guarantee deposit of $100.

Halbart requires that its couriers be at least 18 years of age and have a U.S. passport. No frequent flyer credit is available through Halbart for any of their flights, but you can always try to deal directly with the airlines involved to see if you can get credit.

Recently, the following destinations in Western Europe were being offered:

Destination (Airline)	Departure Days	Length of Stay	Fare Range
Amsterdam	Monday to Friday	One week	$250 - $350
Brussels	Monday to Saturday	One week	$250 - $350
Copenhagen	Monday to Thursday & Saturday	One week	$250 - $350
Frankfort	Monday to Saturday	One week	$150 - $250
London	Monday to Saturday	One week	$250
Madrid	Monday to Saturday	One week	$250 - $350
Milan	Monday to Thursday & Saturday	Two weeks	$300 - $400
Paris	Monday to Thursday & Saturday	One week	$300 - $400
Rome	Tuesday to Thursday & Saturday	One week	$300 - $400
Stockholm	Tuesday to Thursday & Saturday	One week	$250 - $350
Zurich	Monday to Thursday & Saturday	One week	$250 - $300

Policies and Procedures

Flight information is available from 8:00 a.m. to 5:00 p.m. EST, Monday through Friday. Ask for courier information. After hours, an automated attendant will provide you with a list of currently available cities but no information on flight availability or fares. You can also leave a message for a courier representative on this system.

Generally, you can expect to book your flight four to six weeks in advance, although flights are sometimes available on shorter notice. Halbart has a special deal for the last-minute traveler. Call and leave your name and number and the dates you are available to fly. They will call you if there is a last-minute opening. If it's the day before the flight, the fare will be $150 round-trip. The fare drops to $100 round-trip the day of the flight. You must be willing to accept whichever destination opens up. According to Rudy Halbart, there are more than 100 people on the list at any given time.

From time to time, you may have an "open ticket" on your return flight. In other words, you will not be accompanying a courier shipment, which means that the usual allotment of two pieces of checked luggage will be available to you on the return journey. Shoppers take note! Make sure to ask about this when you book your flight.

Intermail Courier

91-06 23rd Avenue
East Elmhurst, NY 11369
(718) 898-2526
(718) 898-9557
Intermail still uses freelance couriers but no longer books them direct. They are referring enquiries to Courier Travel Service (see above).

When you call, ask about Intermail's London options. Round-trip fares were recently $399 for stays of from seven to 30 days. For an extra $50, you can stay for up to three months. Flights are daily except Sunday, and three couriers are used each day.

International Bonded Couriers (IBC)
140-35 Queens Boulevard
Jamaica, NY 11413
(800) 848-9954
(718) 526-5300
(718) 526-2300
(718) 262-8058 (Fax)
I have a soft spot in my heart for IBC because it was for them that I took my very first courier flight. Unfortunately, they had only one route from New York — to London — and they suspended that service during the Persian Gulf War.

"There were just too many problems," they told me, "so now we're dealing directly with the carriers." They tell me, however, that they may be reviving their London service in the future as well as some London flights from Miami.

See the IBC-Pacific listing under Los Angeles for information on their courier service to the Orient, which is still going strong.

Jet Services USA, Inc.
149-21 177th Street
Jamaica, NY 11434
(718) 917-7900
An affiliate of Jet Services in Montreal, Jet Services USA uses on-board couriers, but only if your travel originates from London or Paris into New York. Jet Service's phone number in London is (081) 759-4991; in Paris, (01) 48626222.

Jupiter Air, Ltd. (MICOM America, Inc.)
160-23 Rockaway Boulevard
Jamaica, NY 11434
(718) 341-2095
(718) 527-3763 (Fax)
Jupiter Air has three U.S. locations, New York, San Francisco, and Los Angeles.

Out of New York, Jupiter Air flies to Hong Kong only six times each week. The fare (or as Jupiter prefers to call it, "the administrative fee") is $641 round-trip which is valid year-round. They offer flexible stays from seven days to one month and you can check one piece of luggage in addition to your carry-on allotment. Flights leave Tuesday through Saturday and are usually booked two months in advance; the farthest ahead you can book is three months.

Flights can be booked right over the phone. Once you have booked a flight you must provide payment in full within fourteen days or the booking will automatically be cancelled. Payment must be in cash or by cashier's check. You must also provide a $200 return-guarantee deposit and pay a $35 "life-time membership fee" which is valid for travel from any of Jupiter's U.S. locations.

It may be possible to book through to Bangkok from New York (or from San Francisco or Los Angeles). This would involve making a connection in Hong Kong to another courier flight, which in turn might mean a layover of a day or so in Hong Kong. This is by no means a sure thing but if you're interested call and ask Ms. Sunkyn Cruz if Jupiter can accommodate you.

Once you're in Hong Kong, you can deal directly with the Jupiter office there for courier flights to Bangkok or elsewhere. I'm told that there might be a possibility of getting a Jupiter courier flight from Hong Kong to Tokyo (on JAL flight 734). Most of the courier flights out of Hong Kong, however, seem to use Hong Kong-based Jupiter staffers as couriers. Still, it never hurts to ask. Obviously, if you took any courier flights from Hong Kong, you'd have to arrange to return to Hong Kong in time to fulfill your obligation as a courier on the Jupiter flight back to the United States.

If you're available to travel at the last minute, ask to be put on their emergency waiting list. If a cancellation occurs, they will tell you, you may be offered a fare as low as $250 round-trip. That's the official line, however. Privately I'm told that when they have a last-minute cancellation the administrative fee is waived altogether for whoever steps in to make the flight.

Some of the paperwork you receive from Jupiter may bear the business name, MICOM America. Jupiter Air is headquartered in Hong Kong and is a subsidiary of Japan Air. MICOM America is their U.S. franchisee. The contract they have you fill out, however, says Jupiter Air.

See the San Francisco and Los Angeles listings for information on other Jupiter operations with flights to the Orient.

Now Voyager
74 Varick Street, Suite 307
New York, NY 10013
(212) 431-1616
(212) 334-5243 (Fax)
Founded in 1984, Now Voyager is the oldest New York booking agency. Like the other booking agents, Now Voyager serves a number of different courier companies and offers flights to Europe, the Orient, and South America, giving you one of the broadest selections available.

Unlike the other major booking agencies in New York, Now Voyager charges a $50 annual registration fee. They justify this by pointing out that they mark up their fares less than do other booking agencies. "When we were offering flights to the Caribbean, we were selling them for $50," points out Now Voyager owner, Julie Weinberg. "The other booking agents were charging $99 for these flights—when they could get them. So if it was your first flight, you were paying the same fare. But if it was your second flight with us, you were saving $50." Indeed, the registration fee becomes less of an issue the more frequently you fly. As an educated consumer, you will have to do some comparison shopping and decide for yourself.

Here is a chart showing their European destinations. The fares quoted are the generally available fares, which fluctuate with the seasons and other supply and demand factors. Like other courier companies, Now Voyager discounts fares as the flight date approaches. For example, if the "generally available" fare is $250, Now Voyager may drop that to $199 or $150 if the flight is leaving in less than a week. They once offered a last-minute trip to Hong Kong for free! During the war in the Gulf, there was a spate of $99 round-trip fares to just about every European destination.

Destination	Departure Days	Length of Stay	Fare Range
Amsterdam	Call	One week	$199 - $325
Brussels	Call	One week	$199 - $399
Copenhagen	Call	One week	$150 - $299
Frankfort	Call	One week	$150 - $399
Geneva	Call	One week	$150 - $299
London	Call	One week; up to 30 days	$199 - $350

Destination	Departure Days	Length of Stay	Fare Range
London (from Miami)	Call	One week	$250 - $399
London (from Houston)	Call	Up to 30 days	$275 - $399
Madrid	Call	One week	$199 - $399
Madrid (from Miami)	Call	One week	$250 - $399
Milan	Call	One week; two weeks	$250 - 550
Paris	Call	One week; two weeks	$250 - $399
Rome	Call	8 or 9 days	$250 - $550
Stockholm	Call	One week	$199 - $350
Zurich	Call	One week	$250 - $399

The following South American and Far Eastern destinations are also offered:

Destination	Departure Days	Length of Stay	Fare Range
Buenos Aires	Call	8 to 9 days	$399 - $499
Caracas	Call	5 to 9 days	$175 - $220
Rio	Call	8 to 9 days	$399 - $630
Santiago	Call	8 to 13 days	$499
Mexico City	Monday to Saturday (2 dep. daily)	One week; up to 30 days	$150 - $210
Hong Kong	Call	Two weeks; up to 30 days	$399 - $660

125

Destination	Departure Days	Length of Stay	Fare Range
Tokyo	Call	Two weeks; up to 30 days	$275 - $460
Tokyo (from Houston)	Call	3 to 30 days	$375
Singapore	Call	Two weeks	$399

Where more than one length of stay is given in the above charts, Now Voyager offers two distinct and separate runs. In other words the listing "One week; two weeks" means you can stay *either* one week *or* two weeks but not ten or twelve days. Please be aware that, as with so much in the courier business, these destinations and fares are subject to change.

Now Voyager has recently begun to offer non-courier flights to destinations like Sydney, Bangkok, Singapore, and Europe as well as non-courier domestic flights to Los Angeles, San Francisco, and Miami.

In the past, Now Voyager offered courier flights to Dublin, Athens, Helsinki, Bangkok, Seoul, Los Angeles, New York (from Los Angeles), and to various Caribbean destinations. I mention them here because they may, repeat *may*, offer them again at some time in the future.

One of the best things about Now Voyager is that they have an unusually complete "automated attendant" on their line, which means that you have access to recorded information about flight availability, fares, and Now Voyager policies and procedures 24 hours a day. "We update our recording on specials about four or five times a day," says owner Weinberg. "We're constantly getting calls from courier companies saying, 'We just lost our courier; can you put the flight on your tape?'"

You can also bypass the automated attendant and get a human being during business hours (which are from 11:00 a.m. to 5:30 p.m. EST, Monday through Friday, and Saturdays from 12:30 to 4:30 p.m.) by pressing "0" at any time.

You need to be calling from a touch tone phone to use the automated system. Here's how it works:

Level One. During the initial message you will be prompted to press "2" for faster service. This takes you to . . .

Level Two. Here you will be offered the following menu of choices:

Press 1 — Flight and fare information.
Press 2 — General information about becoming a courier.
Press 3 — To check in for a flight you have already booked.
Press 4 — Information on flight deposits previously made.
Press 5 — Information on cancelling a flight you have booked.
Press 6 — For an operator.

You will probably be most interested in the most recent flight information. When you press "1" you will reach . . .

Level Three. Here you will be given the following menu choices:

Press 1 — Last-minute specials.
Press 2 — Next available flights to Europe.
Press 3 — Next available flights to destinations other than Europe — in other words, South America and the Orient.

To speed through the system to get to the flight information you want (and to save a bit on your long distance bill if you are calling from out of town), do the following: Press "2" then "1" then either "1", "2", or "3" (Last-minute, Europe, elsewhere). So, to hear the last-minute specials the sequence would be 2 - 1 - 1; for flights to the Orient, the sequence would be 2 - 1 - 3, and so forth. You have to wait until you hear the recorded voice at each level before pressing the next number in the sequence.

Once you listen to, say, the recording on last-minute specials, there is no prompt on the system to tell you how to listen to information on next available flights to Europe without making another call. Here's how: when you want to move from one flight information "box" to another, press "0 - 1" in quick succession. This will get you to a variation of the Level Two menu. On this menu, the choice for flight and fare information is "2" which gets you back to the Level Three menu.

Here is a tip on using the recorded information line: tape record it! I have found it impossible to write down all the information they give you — they simply talk too fast.

You can buy a simple, inexpensive hook up that lets you record off your phone from Radio Shack or some similar electronics supply store. Once you've recorded the message, you can replay it and stop it from time to time to allow you to transcribe the information. And don't worry, it's perfectly legal.

Policies and Procedures
As noted above, the Now Voyager recording provides you with information on their policies and procedures. Here are some relevant quotes from that recording:

"To reserve a flight, you must tell us where or when you want to travel. If a courier is needed that day, we book you on that flight and your payment must be made within three business days. We accept cash, money orders, or certified checks as well as

MasterCard, Visa, and American Express. It is slightly less expensive to use cash. We do not accept personal checks.

"A non-refundable registration fee of $50 is required for first-time couriers and is good for one year. If you cancel four weeks prior to your international flight or two weeks prior to your domestic flight, you will be entitled to a 50 percent refund. Some flights may also require a refundable deposit.

"We book as much as two months in advance. For each destination, we generally book one person per flight. If you are booking for more than one person, they will probably have to fly on consecutive days."

By "slightly less expensive to use cash," they mean that they will add a percentage to the cost of your flight to cover the fees charged by the credit card companies. It's two percent for Visa and MasterCard, four percent for Carte Blanche and Diner's Club, and five percent for American Express. Domestic flights (to Los Angeles) are offered only infrequently.

Once you have flown with Now Voyager a few times, you can ask them to put you on a list for last-minute flight when you're available to travel on short notice. "We get calls like that all the time," says Ms. Weinberg, and they pay attention, too. "Especially when we get to know them and they become reliable to us — in other words when we know they're really going to follow through and take a flight. We bandy names around the office all the time."

POLO Express
160-23 Rockaway Boulevard
Jamaica, NY 11434
(718) 527-5546
This company, the New York branch of the much larger London

operation, uses freelance, on-board couriers to Tokyo and London. They have assigned Now Voyager (see above) as their sole booking agent.

POLO's New York office cannot assist you in booking courier flights out of London. POLO also has a presence in San Francisco and Los Angeles (see below).

Priority Air Freight NY, Ltd.
130-29 135th Avenue
South Ozone Park, NY 11420
(718) 529-1600
(718) 529-1657 (Fax)
Priority's New York office co-loads with Halbart (see above). That is, when they have courier pouches to send they turn them over to Halbart which will then book you to accompany them to London. Their London office (see below) sometimes has need of last-minute couriers to New York.

Rush Courier
481 49th Street
Brooklyn, NY 11220
(718) 439-9043
Flies to San Juan, Puerto Rico, Mondays through Thursdays and Saturdays. The fare is $200 round-trip, slightly higher during the Christmas season. There is a minimum stay of three days and a maximum of 21 days. You may take one piece of checked luggage.

Flights generally fill up two to three months in advance. Once you have booked a flight, you must pay in full by cash or money order. If you can (or have to) travel on short notice you may be able to get one of their "rare" cancellations. However, you will not get a break on the fare. Ask for Eileen Martinez.

Shigur/Cosell
147-40 184th Street
Jamaica NY 11413
(718) 244-7356
(718) 244-7870 (Fax)
or
210 East 36th Street
New York, NY 10016
(212) 213-0036
Flies to Israel only. They suspended the use of on-board couriers in August of 1991 and tell me they "have no idea" whether or not they will use them again in the future.

SOS International Courier
8715 La Tijera Boulevard
Los Angeles, CA 90045
(310) 649-6640
(310) 649-1214 (Fax)
This LA-based operation offers six flights each week from New York to Mexico City. The fare is $150 round-trip. Flights leave from JFK via Aeromexico on Mondays through Fridays and on Sundays. You can stay up to 30 days, depending on the availability of return flights. If there is a last-minute opening they may cut the fare by 50% or even offer a free flight, according to SOS's Milton Reyes.

All booking arrangements are handled out of LA. Payment can be made by personal check. Ask to speak with Margie or Dora. See the Los Angeles listing, below, for more information.

TNT Express Worldwide
990 Stewart Avenue
Garden City, New York 11530
(516) 745-9000
TNT employs 10,000 people in 1,200 offices around the world.

Needless to say, that makes them a major player in the air courier game. Unfortunately, TNT's use of on-board couriers has been declining steadily. Out of New York, they fly their own fleet of planes and also co-load with Halbart (see above).

Avid couriers may still want to keep TNT in mind. (See Chapter Eight.)

Trans-Air System
7264 NW 25th Street
Miami, FL 33122
(305) 592-1771
(305) 592-2927 (Fax)
This Miami-based operation used to offer flights from New York to Guatemala and Costa Rica. At press time, these flights had been discontinued. Naturally, there's always the possibility that this service may be restored. You may want to check in from time to time to see.

World Courier, Inc.
137-42 Guy R. Brewer Boulevard
Jamaica, NY 11434
(718) 978-9552, 978-9400
(718) 276-6932 (Fax)
(718) 978-9408 (recorded message line)
(800) 221-6600
As the second edition goes to press, World uses freelancers to Milan and Mexico City only.

They charge a $200 non-refundable "administration fee" for the round-trip travel to Milan. Flights leave Monday, Tuesday, Wednesday, and Thursday and the stay in Milan is seven days — that is, if you leave on a Monday, you return on a Monday. You will be allowed to check one piece of luggage (in addition to your carry-on) on all flights.

The Milan flights, going and coming, require a connection in Amsterdam. On the outbound journey, the connection is immediate; coming back, there is a layover of several hours.

Flights to Mexico, which were added just as the second edition was going to press, depart Sunday through Thursday for an eight day stay. Initially, flights to Mexico were free but by the time you read this World will most likely have implemented plans to charge a fee "in the $100 range" for the Mexico run.

World requires that you have an American or EEC (Common Market) country passport, with a valid "green card" (Permanent Resident Card) in the latter case. Calls for information are accepted Monday through Friday between 9 a.m. and 12 noon, EST. You can call (718) 978-9408 at any time and hear a brief message about current destinations. You can leave your name and address on this line and World will send you additional information and an application. The material they send out to would-be couriers notes that new destinations may become available from time to time.

You must show up at World's offices (as opposed to the airport) on the day of the flight; you **cannot** leave your car in their lot. They will provide you with information on how to get there via public transportation.

World seems most comfortable booking flights well in advance. If they have an open seat on a flight leaving in a week or two, they may lower their fees. I have heard of couriers flying to Milan for as little as $100 round-trip with fairly ample notice. If you are able to travel at the last minute and a cancellation occurs, World will waive their fee! That means you will pay only the applicable departure taxes for your round-trip journey. You must have traveled with World at least once, however, to be eligible for this benefit.

World used to offer on-board courier slots to freelancers on runs to London, Frankfort, and Zurich. During the war in the Persian Gulf, flights to London and Zurich ended—at least for freelancers. Apparently, increased security measures on the other end made using on-board couriers more of a hassle than it was worth. More recently, World stopped offering freelancers flights to Frankfort. The courier business being what it is, however, all this may change. In fact, World seems to change destinations and fees more often than most courier companies; it wasn't too long ago that the fare to Milan was $300! You can check in periodically on their recorded message line to monitor current destinations (but not fares).

World is a "retailer." That is, they are sending packages for their own customers, not someone else's. Originally, World let couriers fly for free. They began charging for their flights, according to one industry insider not connected with World, because too many couriers were not showing up for the return flight. Their decision to use paid employees on many of their runs may reflect continuing problems with unreliable freelancers.

The lesson to be learned for folks like you and me is, "Be reliable." The more problems you cause the courier companies, the more you jeopardize this low-cost travel strategy for everyone.

MIAMI

Because of the large number of retirees in the Miami area, Miami's courier companies have a large pool of willing couriers who are available to travel at a moment's notice. This has the beneficial effect of making courier companies very open to the idea of keeping lists of last-minute travelers. On the down side, it means that the competition for the relatively small number of last-minute slots is quite stiff. Most of the courier companies who maintain lists tell me they are quite long.

If you are a Florida-based senior citizen, who would like to take advantage of the last-minute travel bargains offered by courier travel, by all means get on these lists. I have no information to prove it, but I rather suspect that companies looking for last-minute couriers are more likely to call on people who have flown with them before. So it may be worthwhile to take a regular flight or two before putting yourself forward as an emergency replacement.

AAA International

1641 NW 79th Avenue
Miami, FL 33126
(305) 593-1400
(305) 477-0850 (Fax)
Flies to Costa Rica and other Latin American destinations. They stopped using on-board couriers "about a year ago" but owner Jeff Cordover tells me that they may begin to use them again at some point in the future.

A-1 International

6930 NW 12th Street
Miami, FL 33126
(305) 594-1184
(305) 594-2967 (Fax)
Specializes in Venezuela. They recently offered a stay of up to

· three months in Caracas for $306 round-trip. You may take one 70-pound piece of checked luggage for no extra charge. Bookings can be made up to three months in advance. After hours, their phone carries a recorded message giving background information on the company and the services it offers.

A-1 also offers one-way fares for $200. That means you could go to South America for an open-ended stay and hope for a one-way slot (because of a no-show courier most likely) from one of the contacts listed in "Other Overseas Contacts" to get you back to the States.

A-1 flies to other destinations in the Caribbean and Latin America but at present uses on-boards only on the Caracas run.

Airhitch
2790 Broadway, Suite 100
New York, NY 10025
(212) 864-2000
Listed here because they occasionally offer flights to Europe from Miami. See the New York listing for complete details.

Courier Travel Service
530 Central Avenue
Cedarhurst, NY 11516
(516) 374-2299
(800) ASK-2FLY
(800) 922-2FLY
(516) 374-2261 (Fax)
Courier Travel Service is currently booking for two European destinations out of Miami—London and Madrid. London flights and depart Mondays through Saturdays for a one-week stay only. The fare varies between $299 and $399 depending on the time of year.

Flights to Madrid leave Tuesday through Saturday on Iberia Airlines. Again, the stay is for one week only and the fare is from $299 to $399.

They may also begin booking flights from Miami to South American destinations. See the New York listing for more information on CTS's policies and procedures.

Discount Travel International
152 West 72nd Street
New York, NY 10023
(212) 362-8113
This New York booking agent can put you on flights from Miami to London and Madrid. Flights to London leave Tuesday to Saturday. The stay is for one week and the round-trip fare is $250. There are four flights a week to Madrid on Tuesday, Wednesday, Thursday, and Saturday. Again, the stay is one week and the fare is $250.

There are plans to open a Miami office in the near future so that they can service South American destinations as well. Check Miami information or call their New York office for an update.

Halbart Express
2471 NW 72nd Avenue
Miami, FL 33122
(305) 593-0260
(305) 593-0158 (Fax)
This is a new operation for Halbart (see their New York listing, above), offering service to London and Madrid. There are six flights a week to London, Mondays through Saturday, and four flights to Madrid, on Tuesday, Wednesday, Thursday, and Saturday.

The round-trip fares to London vary from $200 to $250; to

Madrid they range from $200 to $300. "It's a pure supply and demand thing," explains Regional Manager Tom Belmont. "Say next week I still need four couriers out of the nine slots I have. That's a lot. I would cut the price to get couriers for those flights."

As with most courier companies, you can reserve a flight over the phone, but it won't be considered booked until Halbart receives payment by cash, personal check, cashier's check, or money order. If the flight is less than 14 days away and you can't get to their offices in person, you will have to send your payment by overnight mail. Once your flight is paid for, they will send you a contract and instructions on your courier duties.

"We also maintain lists of potential couriers who can travel on 24-hours notice or less," Tom says, "in which case they can pay anywhere from zero to $100." Tom says these people fall into two broad categories. One is Florida-based retirees. "Then there are other people who've traveled as couriers before," says Tom, "who will call and say 'I'm on the swing shift and I can trade some days, so if you have anything going out, give me a call.'"

Tom is one of the nicest people I've come across in the courier business. He obviously takes pride in helping people out. "Because I'm a smaller operation," Tom explains, "I can offer a more personalized service to the courier."

Halbart may expand its Miami operation in the near future to serve the South American market.

International Bonded Courier, Inc.
1771 NW 79th Avenue
Miami, FL 33126
(305) 591-8080
(305) 591-2056 (Fax)
This is the same IBC that flies out of New York and Los Angeles.

This branch covers South America but couriers on these routes are currently full-time employees based in the various cities to which IBC flies. As I keep saying, policies change so they might be worth a call, just in case.

Intertrade Courier International
7370 NW 36th Street, Suite 128
Miami, FL 33166
(305) 592-1700
(305) 592-7952 (Fax)
They are both a wholesaler and a retailer with branch offices throughout Latin America. They serve as an independent service contractor for Federal Express in Columbia, Ecuador, Peru, Paraguay, and Bolivia.

The destinations they serve out of Miami, according to Intertrade's Augusto, are Bogota, Quito, Guayaquil, Caracas, Lima, Buenos Aires, Santiago, Panama City, Rio, Mexico City, Asuncion, Montevideo, and La Paz.

They do none of their own booking of on-board couriers. Instead, they have turned over that responsibility to Line Haul Services (see below) and some other contractors.

LAC Express
Box 523874
Miami, FL 33152
(305) 871-4737
(305) 876-0027 (Fax)
LAC flies to Bogota six days a week. Usually they use their own personnel on this run but if they need someone to go at the last minute, you can go for free. The only catch is, it's a one-way ticket. Getting back will be your own responsibility. If you are interested in this deal, call Raul DeLeon when you can leave on a last-minute, emergency basis and leave your phone number.

Line Haul Services
formerly Carrier A Bordo (CAB)
7859 NW 15th Street
Miami, FL 33126
(305) 477-0651
(305) 599-2002 (Fax)
Line Haul is a wholesale courier company with broad coverage of South and Central America. They also serve as a booking agent for other courier companies.

Currently, they are offering flights to the following cities:

Destination	Departure Days	Length of Stay	Fare Range
Buenos Aires	Daily	Up to 21 days or one month	$450 - $550
Caracas	Monday to Thursday & Saturday	14 days	$250 - $280
Rio	Daily	Up to 21 days or one month	$450 - $550
Santiago	Daily	Up to one month	$450 - $550
Costa Rica	Saturday	Up to one year	$200
Guayaquil	Monday to Thursday	Up to 21 days	$250 - $280
Quito	Monday to Thursday	Up to 21 days	$250 - $280
Lima	Monday to Thursday & Saturday	15 days	$250 - $280
Santo Domingo	Monday to Thursday	One or two weeks	$120

Destination	Departure Days	Length of Stay	Fare Range
Guatemala	Daily	Up to 21 days	$120 - $150
Panama City	Daily	Up to 21 days	$200 - $250

The fare ranges represent high and low season fares. Be aware that length of stay on some runs may vary according to the day of your flight.

Reservations can be made on the phone; call at least three weeks in advance of your travel. Payment can be made by cash, certified check, or money order. They will accept personal checks more than a month before the flight date. No credit cards. Couriers need be only 18, with a valid passport from anywhere.

Line Haul maintains a list of last-minute couriers who live in the Miami area. Apparently the list is large but worth a try if you can pick up and go on short notice.

Now Voyager
74 Varick Street, Suite 307
New York, NY 10013
(212) 431-1616
(212) 334-5243 (Fax)
Another New York booking agency offering flights to London and Madrid out of Miami. Fares on the London run range from $199 to $399, depending on the season and other demand factors. To Madrid, fares range from $250 to $399. There is a one-week stay at each destination.

See the New York listing for more information on Now Voyager's policies and procedures.

Rapid International
6595 NW 36th Street, Suite 109C
Miami, FL 33166
(305) 871-8342
Not using freelancers at this time. Has four full-time couriers on staff.

Security Air Couriers
7311 NW 12th Street, Suite 18
Miami, FL 33126
(305) 477-8633
(305) 477-1211 (Fax)
This company flies to Santiago, Chile, but at this time all their couriers originate in Santiago.

Skynet Worldwide Courier Network
4405 NW 73rd Avenue
Miami FL 33166
(305) 477-0996
(305) 477-0998 (Fax)
Skynet relies primarily on Line Haul (see above) to fill its needs for on-board couriers. However, from time to time they will get couriers on their own, according to vice-president George Iglesias. Usually that means they will turn to their own staff members or to others in the Miami courier business.

Avid couriers in the Miami area may want to write to Skynet indicating their interest and availability.

SOS International Courier
8715 La Tijera Boulevard
Los Angeles, CA 90045
(310) 649-6640
(310) 649-1214 (Fax)
At press time, this LA-based operation was in the planning stages

for a Miami to Mexico City courier run to be instituted sometime in 1992. See the Los Angeles listing, below, for more information.

TNT Express Worldwide

7400 NW 19th Street, Suite E
Miami, FL 33126
(305) 594-2221

TNT's Miami office used to use on-board couriers to South America, but no more, reports TNT staffer Jerry Starr. They have worked out an arrangement with the airlines that allows them to ship unaccompanied baggage at air courier rates. This baggage is then checked through customs with the regular passengers' baggage. According to Starr, the move was made because of custom's increasing worry about drug smuggling. Apparently, the feeling is that unaccompanied shipments are less likely to present contraband problems.

TNT still uses couriers on flights from Miami to Europe but, alas, they are not using freelancers. Instead, they tell me, they rely on either their own people or an airline employee to fill that function. I suspect they may also co-load with Halbart.

Trans-Air System

7264 NW 25th Street
Miami, FL 33122
(305) 592-1771
(305) 592-2927 (Fax)

Trans-Air has courier flights to Guatemala and Costa Rica for $190 round-trip, with stays of up to a year. All flights are on Aviateca Airlines, with the Guatemala flights leaving Sunday through Friday. Flights to Costa Rica leave only on Sunday.

Recently, they added a run to Quito, Ecuador, with flights (via American Airlines) leaving Sunday through Thursday for a stay

143

of up to 21 days. The round-trip fare varies from $180 to $250.

Because Costa Rica is a popular destination and there is only one flight each week, they have devised a strict regimen for booking the few available flights. You must call on the third Monday of the month to book flights two months in advance. In other words, if you are interested in flying on a Sunday in January, you must call on the third Monday in November. It may be worth a call anyway to make sure the system hasn't changed.

Flights to Guatemala are easier to come by. A recent inquiry turned up three available flights in the next two weeks.

Fares to Guatemala and Costa Rica are the same year-round. A non-refundable $50 deposit is required to hold your flight, or you may pay in full. Payment can be in cash or by personal check.

CHICAGO
Courier possibilities out of Chicago are shrinking. In the last edition of *The Insiders Guide To Air Courier Bargains* several companies offering runs to England were featured. TNT is now using British Airways' Speedbird Courier on this run and on-board couriers are booked out of London.

DHL Worldwide Express
5535 Milton Parkway
Rosemont, IL 60018
(708) 678-7169
(708) 678-7160
(708) 678-0541 (Fax)
DHL used to use freelance couriers out of Chicago to London and Mexico City. They now say they have discontinued that program. Still, I hear persistent rumors that DHL, at least occasionally, still uses freelancers.

If you are in the Chicago area — and especially if you are available to travel on short notice — it may be worth dropping a line to "Courier Operations" signalling your interest and availability in serving as a freelance, last-minute, on-board courier.

Leisure Marketing Corporation
2725 North Thatcher Avenue, Suite 210
River Grove, IL 60171
(708) 453-7300
Tim Atkins is the booking rep for TNT Express Worldwide (see below). There are four flights a week to Mexico City, Monday through Thursday evenings, at $200 round-trip. These flights are on Mexicana Airlines (sorry, no frequent flyer mileage) and carry an "open return." For practical purposes, that means you can stay for up to six months.

Call Tim with the dates you want to travel. Once you have arranged a date, you will receive an application which you must return with your payment. You can book "up to three or four months" in advance.

TNT Express Worldwide
4309 Transworld Drive
Schiller Park, IL 60176
(708) 671-9400
Call Leisure Marketing Corporation to book your flights. This number is included just in case Leisure Marketing stops booking TNT flights.

HOUSTON

Fewer and fewer courier possibilities exist out of Texas. Eduardo Trivino of Fast Courier Service in Houston explains, "We used to use [on-board couriers] so we could ship as baggage. But now the airlines are changing their philosophy and they're accepting our shipments as baggage but without the person on board."

Flights to London out of Dallas, which were listed in the last edition, are no longer available. When they were, they were booked by some New York booking agents. You may want to check with them periodically, just in case this run is revived.

International Bonded Courier (IBC)
3050 McKauhan Street
Houston, TX 77032
(713) 821-1900
(Note: When there is no one in the Houston office, calls to this number are forwarded to IBC's Miami office)
IBC's Houston operation has flights to Mexico City but, at least for now, the on-board couriers originate in Mexico.

Now Voyager
74 Varick Street, Suite 307
New York, NY 10013
(212) 431-1616
(212) 334-5243 (Fax)
Now Voyager books flights from Houston to both London and Tokyo. In each case the stay can be for up to 30 days. Round-trip fares to London vary from $275 to $399. Round-trip fares to Tokyo were recently quoted at $375.

All arrangements can be made by mail and/or over the phone with any major credit card. See the New York listing for more information.

TNT Express Worldwide
16544 Air Center Boulevard
Houston, TX 77032
(713) 443-2020
(713) 230-6125 (Fax)
Ships every day to London and Mexico City via Continental Airlines. However, in the case of London they have a special arrangement with the airline to expedite their cargo without the need for an on-board courier. To Mexico they use returning couriers from IBC.

Avid couriers who are interested in the very slim possibility of last-minute courier openings may want to drop TNT a line. Remember, too, that policies may change.

SAN FRANCISCO
Focus On Travel
155 Bovet Road, Suite 150
San Mateo, CA 94402
(800) 722-3246
(415) 571-0323
Focus On Travel is a full-service travel agency that does all the ticketing for IBC-Pacific's flights out of Los Angeles (see below). They can provide you with up-to-date information on IBC's fares and destinations but you will still have to call Los Angeles to get flight availability and book your flight. And you can't pick up your ticket from Focus on Travel, either. That will have to wait until you actually get to the Los Angeles airport.

So why bother calling? Since they're doing the ticketing for IBC, they'll be more than happy to help you with your hotel reservations in IBC's destination cities. They tell me they deal with several Asian hotel wholesalers and can offer excellent rates. If you try them, let me know how it turns out.

IBC-Pacific
(415) 697-5985
Flies out of Los Angeles (see below) but their San Francisco number offers recorded information about what they do, how they work, where they fly to, and current round-trip fares. The recording does not list flight availability.

Jupiter Air, Ltd. (MICOM America, Inc.)
JAL Cargo Terminal
North Access Road
San Francisco, CA 94128
(415) 872-6506
(415) 871-4975 (Fax)
San Francisco is Jupiter's main U.S. location; they also have

offices in New York and Los Angeles. Out of San Francisco, they offer flights to Hong Kong, Singapore, and Manila.

There are six flights a week to Hong Kong, Jupiter's hub city for courier flights around the Pacific Rim. Recently the fare was quoted at $571 round-trip with stays of from seven days to one month. You will be allowed one piece of checked luggage on these flights.

There are five flights a week to Singapore with the fare quoted at $581 round-trip. Again, the stays are from seven days to a month. Couriers on these flights are limited to carry-on luggage only.

To Manila there are two separate fares. If you can manage with carry-on baggage only, the fare is $400 round-trip. For an extra $200 you can take two pieces of checked luggage as well, although you may want to check the airline's excess baggage rates to see if you can get a better deal. There are five flights each week and the stays are the same as those in the other destinations.

Flights can be booked up to three months in advance and usually are. Ask to speak with Hayley Liu when you are ready to book. Once you book a flight, they will send you an application, which you must return with the full fare. You must also provide a $200 return-guarantee deposit and pay a $35 "life-time membership fee" which is valid for travel from any of Jupiter's U.S. locations.

Jupiter maintains a list of last-minute couriers in the San Francisco area for Hong Kong. The "fare" can be as low as the $36 departure tax. If you are in the area and can travel at the spur of the moment, this is a list you will definitely want to be on! Your chances of being called will vary with the time of year, according to Jupiter exec, Raymond Ng. "It probably will not happen in

August or September, our peak season," he cautions, "but if you sign up in December, our slow season, we may call you."

It may also be possible to book passage from San Francisco to Bangkok by hooking up with another Jupiter courier flight from Hong Kong. For more on this and other options out of Hong Kong, see the New York listing. See the Los Angeles listing for additional flights to the Orient.

POLO Express
238 Lawrence Avenue, Suite D
South San Francisco 94080
(415) 742-9613
(415) 742-9614 (Fax)
Polo Express bills itself as "agents for United Airlines' courier division." Needless to say, all flights are via United. They have flights from San Francisco to Hong Kong and Singapore every day of the week except Sunday. The fare to both cities is $350 and the stay is two weeks.

There are also daily flights to Bangkok The round-trip fare is $400, which rises to $600 during the Christmas season. There is a two-week stay.

New to the line up is a run to London. Flights leave six days a week for a 14-day stay. Fares, while not set at press time, will probably be in the $350 range. The introductory fare on this run was $199 round-trip, which illustrates the importance of checking in from time to time to find out what's new.

There is also a Polo office in Los Angeles (see below) that offers additional Pacific Rim destinations. You can make bookings for those flights through the San Francisco office.

The San Francisco office also maintains a list of couriers able to travel on short notice, however I am told that you can't expect any tremendous savings. "We may knock off $50 to $100, but that's about it," a spokesman explained. "We really don't have much call for this sort of thing."

TNT Express Worldwide
845 Cowan Road
Burlingame, CA 94010
(415) 692-9600
Offers courier flights from San Francisco to Hong Kong only. London is no longer available. The Hong Kong flights are booked through UTL Travel (see below). There is a two-week turnaround on these flights "which is never flexible." The "fee" charged is $450, plus a $200 return-guarantee deposit which you will get back approximately one month after you return.

When you call to request information, you will be transferred to a recorded announcement which gives a brief overview of the courier program and refers you to the UTL phone number; UTL is not identified by name. At the end of the message you can record your name and address to request an application to be a TNT courier.

UTL Travel
320 Corey Way
South San Francisco, CA 94080
(415) 583-5074
(415) 583-8122 (Fax)
UTL is a booking agent for a number of air courier companies, flying on Singapore Airlines, JAL, and United. They have done away with their annual "membership" fee — good news for the avid courier. Recently, they were offering the following Pacific Rim destinations:

To Hong Kong, there are a total of fifteen flights each week. You can choose a two-week stay at a round-trip fare of $400, or stay for up to 30 days for a fare of $465.

To Singapore, there are ten flights a week. Again, the fare varies according to the length of stay. Two-week stays are $400, while stays of up to 30 days are $465.

To Bangkok, there are five flights a week. The fare is $450 for a two-week stay.

There are four flights a week to Manila, with stays of up to four weeks. If you can restrict yourself to carry-on luggage, the fare is $450. For $550 you can check two pieces of luggage.

New to UTL's line-up is a courier run to London on United with a round-trip fare of $375 for a two-week stay.

All fares quoted will be higher during the summer and at Christmas-time. You can book on the phone but your flight will only be secured when payment is received. If there is more than two weeks before flight time, UTL will accept a personal check. Otherwise, payment must be by cash or money order. UTL accepts bookings up to three months in advance. Some runs require a $100 or $200 return-guarantee deposit, depending on the policy of the courier company.

There is no recorded information line. They prefer it if you call in with specific dates and destinations in mind.

UTL will offer reduced fares if there is a last-minute need for couriers. The fare varies according to courier company policy, but is usually in the $250 range. Steven Tse urges would-be last-minute couriers to provide UTL with their day-time phone numbers. "If we call and get a machine," he warns, "we erase them from the list because we know we won't hear from them until the next day, and that's too late."

From time to time, UTL can offer bookings on courier flights out of Los Angeles. Call and check on availability when you're ready to travel.

Way To Go Travel
1850 Union Street, Suite 6
San Francisco, CA 94123
(415) 292-7801
This booking agency offers two courier runs from San Francisco, to Hong Kong and Singapore. Round-trip fares to both destinations were recently quoted at $425, plus the inevitable tax. Stays are for two weeks exactly. There are five flights each week to each destination, Tuesday through Saturday.

See Way To Go's Los Angeles listing for complete information on their policies and procedures as well as flights to other destinations.

LOS ANGELES
Airhitch
1341 Ocean Avenue
Santa Monica, CA 90401
(310) 458-1006
The Los Angeles office of an enterprising, student-run operation specializing in ultra-low-cost flights to Europe. See the New York listing for complete details on their operation.

Call the Los Angeles office between 7 a.m and 9 a.m. or between 7 p.m. and 9 p.m. PST for more information.

ANZ Travel
25255 Cabot Road
Los Angeles, CA 92653
(310) 379-2483
ANZ stands for Australia, New Zealand. They are a full-service travel agency offering discounted fares to those countries. They used to book couriers on these runs. A recent inquiry revealed that they still have no courier flights available but that they might offer them in the future. Contact the owner, Peter Adam, for an update.

Courier Travel Service
530 Central Avenue
Cedarhurst, NY 11516
(516) 374-2299
(800) ASK-2FLY
(800) 922-2FLY
(516) 374-2261 (Fax)
CTS may be able to book you on courier flights leaving from Los Angeles. See the New York listing for more information on CTS's policies and procedures.

Excalibur International Couriers
6310 West 89th Street
Los Angeles, CA 90045
(310) 568-1000
Excalibur ships cargo to London and a number of Pacific Rim destinations. To London, they have formed a relationship with Virgin Airlines that lets them avoid using couriers. They have also recently dropped their Sydney flights, as couriers on this run now originate in Sydney. They do all their booking to Asian destinations through Way To Go (see below) and seldom, if ever, book couriers directly.

Graph Air Freight
5811 Willoughby Avenue
Hollywood, CA 90038
(213) 461-2719
Graph used to use freelancers but has discontinued the practice as of 1989. Reason: they purchased their tickets so far in advance that they were unable to tell the airlines the name of the passenger who would be accompanying the checked baggage. In this age of terrorism, the airlines balked.

Graph now ships their freight as ordinary, unaccompanied air freight. They tell me they don't anticipate returning to the use of on-board couriers "unless something changes drastically." Don't bother calling them unless you're really desperate.

IBC-Pacific
1595 East El Segundo Boulevard
El Segundo, CA 90245
(310) 607-0125
(310) 607-0126 (Fax)
(415) 697-5985 (recorded information line for LA flights)
IBC-Pacific uses freelance, on-board couriers to several cities in the Orient. Recent destinations and round-trip fares were Tokyo

($350), Hong Kong ($350), Singapore ($425), and Bangkok ($500). Fares don't vary with the season and have remained remarkably stable over the past year or so — in fact, the fare to Hong Kong has actually gone down! A run to Taipei has been discontinued. Apparently, they found it easier to route Taipei-bound cargo via Tokyo or Hong Kong and use agents there to get it to China.

Stays are from 7 to 15 days, depending on your destination and day of departure. Here's how it's been working out recently:

There are seven flights each week to Tokyo. Flights leaving Sunday are for a seven-day stay, those leaving Friday are for 11 days. Flights on all other days are for nine-day stays.

To Hong Kong, there are five flights each week. Tuesday departures are for a 15-day stay while Wednesday and Thursday flight are for nine days. Trips leaving Friday are 11 days, on Saturday for 12 days.

To Singapore, there are five flights a week. Tuesday to Friday departures are for a 14-day stay. Saturday flights are for seven days.

To Bangkok there are five flights a week. Tuesday departures are for 11-day stays. Wednesday and Thursday flights are for 14 days. Friday departures are for 9-day stays while Saturday flights are for 10 days.

From time to time, IBC offers last-minute specials — usually due to a cancellation. They tell me these specials are rare during the summer and unheard of at Christmas time. Your best bet is slower travel months like February or October. Fares may be reduced to half-price or $100. I know of some couriers who report flying free with IBC.

Make sure to ask about frequent flyer mileage when flying with IBC. During a recent four-month period it was possible to get a 10,000 mile bonus on all Northwest flights. This meant that a flight to the Orient would automatically qualify you for a free domestic trip!

Call the (310) number between the hours of 10 a.m. and 3 p.m. PST to get more information and book a flight. They will send you a complete packet of information about their policies and procedures. During other times, the number carries a recorded message giving current destinations and fares (but no information on flight availability). A similar recording can be reached at the (415) number given above; it is located in IBC's corporate offices.

These recordings also spell out IBC policies as follows:

"We require payment in full 14 days prior to departure. We accept reservations for the current month plus the subsequent three months. If you cancel your trip less than 14 days prior to your departure, you forfeit the entire amount for your courier trip.

"All courier flights are round-trip. In order to be absolutely certain that we have the use of your services on the return portion of your courier trip, we require a return-guarantee deposit of $500. This deposit must be submitted in full at the time your contract is processed. We do not accept personal checks for either the trip fee or the return-guarantee deposit. We do accept cash, money orders, cashier's checks, MasterCard and Visa. The return-guarantee deposit is held by us and returned to you upon the successful completion of your courier trip.

"You are not allowed to check any baggage on your courier flight. You may take carry-on baggage only. If you absolutely must take a checked bag you will have to pay the airline the excess baggage charge directly to them."

Jupiter Air (MICOM America)
6041 West Imperial Highway
Building 4, Section E
Los Angeles, CA 90045
(310) 670-5123
(310) 649-2771 (Fax)
Jupiter's Los Angeles operation currently offers courier flights to Hong Kong and Singapore only. Flights to Seoul and Sydney have been discontinued, at least for now. Round-trip fares were recently quoted as $571 to Hong Kong and $581 to Singapore, the same as flights out of San Francisco.

There are six flights each week to each city and you can choose a stay of from seven days to one month. Flights to Hong Kong allow one piece of checked luggage in addition to your carry-on allotment. To Singapore, you may take carry-on luggage only. You must also provide a $200 return-guarantee deposit and pay a $35 "life-time membership fee" which is valid for travel from any of Jupiter's U.S. locations. If you are available to fly at the last minute and they have an opening, they will reduce their fares, they tell me, to $250 round-trip. Ask to speak with Candace Chu when you're ready to book.

It may also be possible to book passage from Los Angeles to Bangkok by hooking up with another Jupiter courier flight from Hong Kong. For more on this and other options out of Hong Kong, see the New York listing. See the San Francisco listing for additional flights to the Orient.

Midnite Express International Couriers
930 West Hyde Park Boulevard
Inglewood, CA 90302
(310) 672-1100
(310) 671-0107 (Fax)
This extremely friendly operation flies to London every Saturday

via United Airlines. Round-trip fares are $500 during the "high" season (from June 1 to September 30 and from *approximately* December 12 to January 1) but drop to $400 during the rest of the year. They book four to six weeks in advance. Your stay in London must be a minimum of one week but you can stay for up to six months.

To fly with Midnite Express you *must* live in Southern California, which is defined as the area bounded by Santa Barbara to the north, Palm Springs to the east, and San Diego to the south. You also must be at least 21 years of age.

If you're in United's frequent flyer program, it's worth going after the mileage credit for this flight. Save your boarding passes. Midnite will take your frequent flyer number but, technically, credit is not allowed on this flight; it's a matter between you and United.

The best time to call for information is between 9 and 10 a.m. PST, Monday through Friday. Ask to speak with Ken Gilbert. Payment can be made on Visa, MasterCard, or American Express.

Now Courier
619 South New Hampshire Avenue
Los Angeles, CA 90005
(310) 671-1200
(213) 252-5070
Now Courier used to the operate courier runs on the New York-L.A. corridor but discontinued them because of economic conditions described earlier.

At press time, they were considering implementing a number of international runs that would require the use of on-board couriers. When they had flights, Now Courier used Now Voyager in New York to book them.

POLO Express
6011 Avion Drive, Suite 204
Los Angeles, CA 90045
(310) 410-6822
(310) 641-2966 (Fax)
Polo offers four Pacific Rim destinations from Los Angeles. All runs allow carry-on baggage only and, according to Polo, they never have any last-minute openings. Personal checks will be accepted for payment if the flight is more than six weeks away. Otherwise, it's the old standbys — cash, cashier's checks, and money orders.

Flights to Hong Kong leave Monday through Saturday. The round-trip fare is $350 with a two-week stay.

There are flights to both Sydney and Melbourne in Australia. There are departures to Sydney every day except Sunday, while flights to Melbourne leave only on Thursdays and Saturdays. The fare to both destinations is $599 round-trip and the stay is three weeks.

New to the line up is service from LAX to London. Flights leave six days a week for a 14-day stay. Regular fares had not been set at press time, but will probably be in the $350 range. The introductory fare on this run was $199 round-trip which, once again, illustrates the importance of checking in from time to time to find out what's new.

Polo also services Bangkok but flights are not available year-round. When they do fly, the fare is $400 and the stay two weeks.

Polo has a San Francisco office (see above) and offers flights from there to London, Hong Kong and Singapore. You can book these flights through the Los Angeles office.

SOS International Courier
8715 La Tijera Boulevard
Los Angeles, CA 90045
(310) 649-6640
(310) 649-1214 (Fax)
SOS offers five flights each week to Mexico City. There are departures Sundays through Thursdays. The fare is $150 round-trip. You can stay up to 30 days, depending on the availability of return flights. If there is a last-minute opening they may cut the fare by 50% or even offer a free flight, according to SOS's Milton Reyes.

American citizens do not need a passport to travel to Mexico, but must present a birth certificate to prove citizenship. SOS requires that couriers other than U.S. nationals have resident alien status in the United States. Payment for your flight can be made by personal check. Ask to speak with Margie or Dora.

SOS also offers flights to Mexico City from New York and plans to institute service from Miami in the near future. All bookings, regardless of point of departure, are handled by the Los Angeles office.

Way To Go Travel
6679 Sunset Boulevard
Hollywood, CA 90028
(213) 466-1126
(213) 466-8994 (Fax)
Way To Go is a booking agency for several air courier companies; there is no registration fee. They offer flights to Hong Kong, Singapore, Kuala Lumpur, Penang, Djakarta, Sydney, and Melbourne from Los Angeles and to Hong Kong and Sydney from San Francisco.

Hong Kong round-trips are $425 with two-week stays. Fares to

Singapore, Kuala Lumpur, and Penang fluctuate with the seasons. To Singapore fares are $490 to $590. To Kuala Lumpur and Penang they vary from $550 to $650. You can stay up to two months at these destinations and for an extra $75 you can extend your stay for up to six months.

Flights to Sydney and Melbourne in Australia were recently quoted at $650 round-trip with a stay of up to three months.

Way To Go books its flights up to six weeks in advance. There is a return-guarantee deposit required for all their South East Asia flights; it is $100 for those holding American passports, $200 for non-U.S. passport holders and $400 for all South East Asian nationals. The deposit is, of course, returned when you return.

The agency also offers a Travel Club which you can join for $75 a year ($150 for a "family membership" including two adults and three children). Members are given first crack at last-minute air courier bargain fares. You may receive up to three days notice of these "last-minute" situations to give you time to FedEx payment. Membership in the Travel Club also entitles you to discounts on regular airfares, car rentals, cruises, railpasses, and such. You don't have to be a member of the club, however, to take advantage of their courier fares.

Bookings will be held only with full payment. They will hold your telephone booking only for 24 hours; it's up to you to get your payment to them A.S.A.P. Personal checks will be accepted two weeks or more prior to the flight; after that, payment must be by cash, certified check, or money order. No credit cards are accepted and no frequent flyer credit is available on any of the tickets they sell.

Way To Go also has a branch in San Francisco, offering flights to Hong Kong and Singapore (see above).

World Travel and Tours
3700 Wilshire Boulevard, Suite 200
Los Angeles, CA 90010
(213) 384-1000
World books on-board couriers for TNT Express Worldwide's LA to Seoul, Korea, run. Until recently, they also handled flights to Singapore and Auckland, New Zealand, for TNT. Couriers for these runs now originate in Auckland and Singapore. That, however, may change, so it might be worth giving World a call to see if any new courier routes are being offered when you want to travel.

Round-trip fares to Seoul were recently quoted at $395, with a stay of two weeks. There are four flights each week. Flights can be booked by phone and must be paid for in cash or by personal check one week before the flight.

Mr. Jang Choi of World Travel tells me that when they need a courier on short notice, they sometimes offer free flights!

ENGLAND

A fter New York, London is probably the main jumping-off point for international courier travel. This account, by our London correspondent, Roger Johansen, should be of particular interest to the dedicated bargain traveler:

"There is a reasonable market for freelance couriers in London, as long as you know where to apply. You can spend a great deal of time telephoning companies listed as courier companies in the Yellow Pages only to find that the majority of them are either motor-cycle dispatch companies or simply air freight companies using the word "courier" to lend added credibility to their operation.

"Of the companies providing their customers with a genuine on-board courier service, the vast majority do not use freelancers because they like to send members of their own staff. It is regarded as a 'perk' of working for such companies to be able to travel at greatly reduced, or zero, cost.

"Most of the 'real' air courier companies are located near Heathrow airport. If you see a courier company listed in, say, Brixton, South London, you can be pretty sure it comprises a bunch of leather-jacketed, motor-cycle messengers.

"There are comparatively few companies that actively recruit freelance couriers, and those tend to book couriers for other companies which don't wish to spend the time finding people to fill their courier slots.

"Finally, a word of advice. Many of the companies that do not book freelancers themselves justify their attitude by saying that it is not worth the trouble, and that they are not prepared to risk the unreliability of freelance couriers. With this latter point in mind, you will do yourself and all others trying to travel economically a service by being reliable, punctual, and as helpful as possible."

Several British couriers have told me that the fares offered by London's courier companies, especially to the United States, are not that much lower than those that can be obtained from the "bucket shops" in London and elsewhere in Britain. These are consolidators (see page 57) and charter operators who specialize in discount air fares.

The following list will get you started. These contacts have been culled from advertisements. I have no personal experience of any of these operations and, naturally, cannot vouch for their reliability. Caveat emptor.

Able Air	(071) 639-7563
Charter Flight Centre	(071) 828-1090
E.L.H. Leisure	(0604) 880510
The Final Frontier	(071) 288-6114
Flight Finders	(071) 938-3933
High Ridings Travel	(0924) 471177
Jenny May Holidays	(071) 228-0321
M & J Travel	(071) 436-8332
Macro Flights	(0402) 476571
Merit Travel	(081) 653-6514

Trendy Travel   (071) 580-5344
World-Wide Flights   (081) 533-0072

There is also a telephone service, Late Savers, that provides information on the availability of last-minute, discounted flights from Gatwick airport. The number is (0898) 505150. There is a charge for this call—it's the British equivalent of a (900) number in the States.

If you are beginning your travel from England, you may want to check out these discount fares. If the difference is only a few pounds, they might be worth taking for the added convenience of a full luggage allotment and a more flexible length of stay. If your time is flexible, you may want to wait for the deeper discounts offered for last-minute courier flights.

If you are arriving from America, these bucket shops can be a source of cheap fares to other European destinations. Many of them offer attractive fares and vacation packages to destinations in Spain, Portugal, and elsewhere in the Mediterranean that are popular with British vacationers.

The dedicated British traveler — and I use the word "traveler" here in the sense of one who goes abroad for an extended period of time — may want to consider the following option: Go to the United States on a cheap air ticket or by some other means that allows you to stay for an extended period of time. Then use courier flights from the U.S. to London when you need to pop home to see Mum or to replenish the exchequer. U.S. to London courier fares tend to be a much better bargain than those in the opposite direction. And I know from experience that last-minute fares from New York (when they are available) offer some truly eye-popping discounts.

Also, as you tour the United States, you can take advantage of

167

courier flights from Miami, Los Angeles, or other gateway cities to expand your travel horizons even further.

Here is a list of companies offering air courier opportunities out of London. I have also listed some companies which have discontinued using freelancers or which book couriers only through agencies, knowing that some of them may change their policies in the future.

You will notice that there are several booking agents, all offering essentially the same flights for somewhat different fares. You will have to weigh fares charged against services offered and make your own determination as to which service to use. Be aware that some agents may be able to put you on flights that others can't. For example, if courier booking agency "A" receives a cancellation for a previously booked flight they may the only ones who can offer that particular seat to you.

As they say in England: "Bon voyage!"

[Note: To dial direct to London from the United States, first dial (011) which tells the phone company you are making an international call. Then dial (44), which is England's "country code." Then dial the numbers listed below.]

Air Action
Unit 5, Christopher Road
Market Trading Estate
Southall
Middlesex UB2 5YG
(081) 573-1857
(081) 573-9372 (Fax)

Air Action used to use freelancers on a run to New York a few years back but now uses its own people when it has a need. There may be a slim, repeat *slim*, possibility of flying with them as a last-minute, emergency replacement.

If you'd like to have a go, your best strategy is to write or fax them, giving your availability. "It might be nice to have some details on file," they told me, "but whether we'd ever use it is something else again."

Bridges Worldwide
114G Building 521
London Heathrow Airport
Hounslow
Middlesex TW6 3UJ
(081) 759-8059
(081) 759-8069 (Fax)
Bridges is a major wholesaler which serves as Virgin Atlantic's ground handling agent.

Some of their courier runs — to the Indian subcontinent, for example—use only professional full time couriers. There are two reasons for this I am told: first, Indian regulations make it problematical to use anyone other than a professional, bonded courier to bring in dutiable cargo and, second, most people wanting to fly from London to India are looking for a lengthy stay, making it necessary to plan bookings very far in advance. They have a run between London and Malta that originates in Malta, using only Maltese citizens, and a run to South Africa that uses a special arrangement with South African Airways that doesn't require an on-board courier.

That still leaves a lot of the world for the on-board courier to see. Check out the Courier Travel Services listing, below, for more information.

City Link International Ltd.
Unit 1, Amberley Way
Hounslow
Middlesex TW4 6BH
(081) 570-3033
(0932) 785-560 (Fax)

City Link is an international courier company that is now using Speedbird (see below) for most of its courier runs. They also use other agents for different parts of the world.

They tell me that "very rarely" they will find themselves in a situation where they need to find their own on-board couriers.

At press time, City Link told me that they were being "bought out" by another company. Should you call, don't be surprised if the operation has a new name.

Courier Travel Services
346 Fulham Road
London SW10 9UH
(071) 351-0300
(071) 844-2666 (Fax)

CTS operates a "Courier Club" using freelance couriers to a large number of destinations. While you must be registered with them, there is no fee charged. CTS provides couriers to British Airways' "Speedbird Express" courier service as well as companies such as TNT, Jet Services, and Bridges Worldwide.

The range of available destinations has shrunk considerably since the first edition. Miami and Mauritius have been added but Bangkok, Dubai, Montreal, Vancouver, Chicago, Houston, Auckland, Bahrain, Singapore, Lisbon, Vienna, Basel, Geneva, and Rome have all dropped from the list. The courier business being the courier business, however, these destinations may crop

170

up again at some time in the future. If you have your heart set on a holiday in Dubai, it may be worth checking in every now and again.

Still, CTS offers a wide range of destinations. One of their more attractive offerings is a weekend getaway to Paris for just £50.

Some recent destinations and round-trip prices were:

Destination	Flights/ Week	Length of Stay	Fare Range
Dallas	6	1, 2, 3, or 4 weeks	£150 - £275
Harare	5	1, 2, 3, or 4 weeks	£375 - £525
Hong Kong	7	1, 2, 3, or 4 weeks	£350 - £575
Johannesburg	2	1, 2, 3, or 4 weeks	£350 - £575
Los Angeles	14	1, 2, 3, or 4 weeks	£199 - £325
Mauritius	2	15 days	£375 - £575
Miami	7	1, 2, 3, or 4 weeks	£150 - £275
Nairobi	3	22 days	£350 - £575
New York	7	1, 2, 3, or 4 weeks	£150 - £275
Paris	1	weekend	£50
Rio	3	1, 2, 3, or 4 weeks	£350 - £525
San Francisco	7	1, 2, 3, or 4 weeks	£199 - £325

Destination	Flights/ Week	Length of Stay	Fare Range
Sydney	7	1, 2, 3, or 4 weeks	£650 - £800
Tokyo	5	1, 2, 3, or 4 weeks	£475 - £550
Toronto	7	1, 2, 3, or 4 weeks	£175 - £299

Unfortunately, Courier Travel Services offers no recorded information line to keep you up-to-date on fares and flight availability to all these destinations. You will simply have to ring them up to find out what's available.

Couriers must be at least 18 years of age and there is no upper age limit. You can book flights up to three months in advance. Once a flight is booked, the courier must complete an application form and pay for the flight before it can be comfirmed. Payment can be by cash, personal check, cashier's check (banker's draft), Visa, or Mastercard and must be received at least seven days before the flight. No return-guarantee deposit is collected. Many CTS destinations allow the courier one piece of checked luggage (up to 23 kilos). Be sure to check the policies on your chosen route when you book your flight.

Like all courier companies, Courier Travel Services sometimes needs couriers on short notice. They tell me they will sometimes reduce the fare for last-minute couriers to their U.S. destinations to £50 round-trip, depending on time of year.

Ask to speak to Keith, David, or Kirsty when you are ready to book. By the way, the London Courier Travel Services is not directly connected with Courier Travel Service in New York although they work together regularly.

DHL International (UK), Ltd.
Orbital Park
178-188 Great South West Road
Hounslow
Middlesex TW4 6JS
(081) 890-9393
(081) 890-9952

DHL's official policy is to use its own employees. When you call, they will tell you that they no longer offer courier flights to the general public. However, DHL may use freelance couriers "in extenuating circumstances." I have heard enough scuttlebut from courier industry insiders to convince me that, at least occasionally, they do.

DHL, after all, is a huge international operation. Even with their large staff (there are over 700 at Orbital Park alone) they must occasionally need outsiders. In New York, for example, DHL occasionally turns to the booking agents to find the odd courier when their internal resources can't meet the demand for on-board couriers.

I suspect their reluctance to advertise the fact that they use outsiders is a marketing decision. They would, for obvious reasons, prefer to give their customers the impression that their valuable documents are firmly in DHL's hands at every step from Point A to Point B.

As for how to get in line for any DHL courier slots that might be available, your guess is as good as mine. Knowing someone at DHL would obviously help. Failing that, and if you live close to Heathrow and are available to travel at short notice (a pensioner or ne'er-do-well student, for example), you may want to write expressing your interest and availability. Do whatever you can in your correspondence to assure them of your trustworthiness and make it easy for them to contact you.

F. B. On-Board Courier
518 Bath Road, Longford
West Drayton
Middlesex UB7 0EZ
(0753) 680280
(0753) 680424 (Fax)

F.B.'s London office offers flights to Montreal and, through Montreal, to Toronto. There is only one flight a week, on Friday evening. The return is 12 days later on Wednesday evening, arriving back in London on Thursday morning. Flights are on Air Canada and couriers are eligible for frequent flyer credit.

Because there are so few flights, you can book up to a year or more in advance; the book opens in November for the following year. Fares vary between £150 and £200 round-trip. Bookings can be made by phone to Sharon Bosson. Tell her the date(s) you wish to travel and, if there's a flight available, she will ask you to send a deposit of at least £50 to hold the flight. She, in return, will send you the courier agreement by return post. Payment in full must be made within two weeks of the flight date.

If you would like to be put on a stand-by list for a last-minute departure, drop a short note to Sharon, giving details on your availability. The day before the flight, the fare drops to £50. "If it's 10:30 at night and I'm really desperate," Sharon says, "it'll go for nothing."

International Bonded Couriers (IBC)
Room 16-20, Building 219
Epsom Square
London Heathrow Airport
Hounslow
Middlesex TW6 2HN
(081) 759-4076
(081) 759-4429 (Fax)

IBC has turned to British Airways' Speedbird service as a way of avoiding the hassles involved in booking their own on-board couriers.

Jet Services London
Unit 5, Phoenix Distribution Park
Phoenix Way
Eston
Middlesex CW5 9ND
(081) 759-4991
(081) 759-4233 (Fax)
This is the London branch of the Jet Services in Montreal and New York. They use freelance couriers but book them exclusively through Courier Travel Services (see above).

Jupiter Air (UK) Ltd.
Unit 4, Pier Road
North Feltham Trading Estate
Feltham
Middlesex TW14 0TW
(081) 751-3323
(081) 751-4773 (Fax)
Jupiter Air's London operation uses freelancers to one destination only: Sydney. A run to Los Angeles has been dropped, at least for now. The round-trip fare to Sydney varies from £800 in the high season to £500. The stay is for up to two months and there are seven flights each week.

Jupiter requires its couriers to be between 18 and 65 years old. Bookings can be made up to three months in advance by phone, letter, or fax. Payment in full must be made two weeks before the flight; cash, personal check, Visa, and MasterCard are accepted.

You will be allowed to take one 20 kilo bag on this run, although oversized items such as surfboards are frowned upon. Jupiter requires no return-guarantee deposit for the Sydney flight. Ask Mel Bromley, Jupiter's European general manager, or Julie Colesell to send you a courier registration form. There is no registration fee.

Line Haul Express
Building 200, Section D
Enfield Road
London Heathrow Airport
Hounslow
Middlesex TW6 2PR
(081) 759-5969
(081) 759-5973 (Fax)
Line Haul is a Hong Kong-based courier company whose London office can put you on flights to Hong Kong. There are some ten to twelve flights each week, depending on the time of year, leaving from both Heathrow and Gatwick airports. The round-trip fare varies from £450 to £500 with stays of up to three months available.

The booking procedure is somewhat unusual. Would-be couriers can phone Line Haul and tell them the dates on which they want to travel. Line Haul then faxes to Hong Kong to enquire about availability; the answer comes back the next day. If they have a ticket for you, they will send you a contract which you send back with payment in full. Payment can be by personal check; no credit cards are accepted.

If your preferred dates are not available, you can ask to be put on a stand-by list in case of a cancellation. This system also works for last-minute travelers. Simply let them know of your availability and they will put you on the stand-by list. If they find themselves in need of your services on a day or two's notice, they will drop the round-trip fare to £200.

Unlike some long-haul courier flights, Line Haul's run to Hong Kong does not allow any checked luggage, just your usual carry-on allotment.

POLO
208 Epsom Square
London Heathrow Airport
Hounslow
Middlesex TW6 2BL
(081) 759-5383
(081) 759-5697 (Fax)
POLO provides couriers to British Airways' Speedbird and a number of other companies. Consequently, they offer a large number of destinations.

If you are interested in a specific destination, you can telephone and inquire about its availability. Otherwise, you can obtain a list of their current offerings by sending a self-addressed, stamped envelope (or international reply coupon, available at the Post Office) to the above address.

At press time, they were serving the following destinations, world-wide:

Destination	Flights/ Week	Length of Stay	Fare Range
Abu Dhabi	6	8 days	£160
Amsterdam	5	3 to 5 days	£39 - £49
Athens	13	1 or 2 weeks	£75 - £95
Bangkok	4	2 weeks	£350
Barcelona	6	1 or 2 weeks	£60
Berlin	5	2 to 7 days	£70
Boston	5	1 or 2 weeks	£135 - £210

Destination	Flights/ Week	Length of Stay	Fare Range
Chicago	6	1 or 2 weeks	£135 - £210
Detroit	5	1 or 2 weeks	£135 - £210
Dubai	1	8 days	£160
Gaborone	2	22 days	£370
Hong Kong	14	2 or 3 weeks	£425
Jersey	5	day return	£25
Jersey	5	2 to 5 days	£39
Johannesburg	7	3 weeks	£475
Kuala Lumpur	4	2 weeks	£315
Lisbon	14	5 to 10 days	£55
Los Angeles	13	1, 2, or 3 weeks	£225 - £325
Miami	7	1 week	£135 - £210
Montreal	1	1 week	£135 -£210
Munich	5	1 week	£70
Nairobi	5	22 days	£300
Newark	6	1 or 2 weeks	£135 - £210
New York	20	1 or 2 weeks	£135 - £210
Philadelphia	6	1 or 2 weeks	£135 - £210
Pittsburgh	1	1 week	£135 - £210
Seattle	5	2 weeks	£199 - £280
Singapore	7	2 or 3 weeks	£335
Sydney	5	26 or 27 days	£600
Tel Aviv	6	1 or 2 weeks	£135
Toronto	6	1 or 2 weeks	£135 - £210
Washington	6	1 week	£135 - £210

The U.S. destinations are available only from London; in other words, you cannot fly from Detroit (say) to London and back. Alas, there is no recorded message line to keep you updated on flights and fares.

Couriers must be 18 years old and in good health. Couriers will not be allowed to travel with children under 13. There is no need to pre-register; when you are ready to book a flight, they will simply ask for your name, address, and telephone number. They recommend booking one to two months in advance. Payment in full is due five days before the flight and can be made by cash, personal check, banker's draft, Visa, or MasterCard. No return-guarantee deposit is required. On some flights, one 23-kilo bag can be checked by the courier.

Polo is very upfront about the supply and demand nature of the courier travel business. The fares quoted above are the "generally available" fares and assume that you will be booking your flight well in advance so Polo can rest assured that the slot is filled. However, not every flight is filled well in advance and cancellations do occur. This opens a window of opportunity for the frugal traveler. "Fares are steadily reduced as the departure dates become closer," they tell me. "Within 24 hours [of flight time] a substantial reduction can be negotiated."

Priority Air Freight, Ltd.
48-49 G, Building 521
Cargo Terminal
London Heathrow Airport
Hounslow
Middlesex TW6 3SP
(081) 759-4422
(081) 897-2613 (Fax)
Priority ships to two destinations in the U.S. — New York and Miami. However, they don't use couriers originating in London.

Instead, they use couriers from Halbart (see the New York and Miami listings) who are returning to their home base.

General manager, Bill Rayner, tells me that every once in a while they run into problems with returning couriers. In fact, the last time I checked in with Priority for a return flight to New York, they told me a courier "had gone sick on us" for a return flight the next day. If you're available in such a situation, you can pick up an open return ticket to New York for £100 (or perhaps less if you decide to drive a hard bargain). The main advantage of an open ticket, of course, is that you can stay as long as you want, which might make it worth the "full" £100 Bill asks.

If you're interested in serving as an emergency replacement, drop Priority a line. It will help, obviously, if you can point out that you live close to Heathrow.

Seabourne Express Couriers
Unit 1, Prescot Road
Poyle Estate, Colnbrook
Slough, Berkshire SL3 0AE
(0753) 683171
Seabourne has absorbed Abacus Couriers, which was listed in the last edition. They tell me they now use only their own staff members "when we need the odd courier." It's considered a perk of employment. If you're interested in becoming a Seabourne employee, contact operations manager Russell Price.

Shades International Travel
Unit 6, Drumhill Works
Clayton Lane
Clayton
West Yorkshire BD14 6RF
(0274) 814727
(0274) 815256 (Fax)

Shades is another booking agent for Speedbird (see below). According to their promotional literature, full luggage allowance is allowed on all flights. They also point out that the Sydney run is via Tokyo, requiring an overnight stay; Speedbird will pick up your hotel tab but no incidental expenses.

They are currently offering bookings to the following destinations:

Destination	Flights/ Week	Length of Stay	Typical Fares
Abu Dhabi	Call	8 days	£190
Amsterdam	”	3 or 5 days	£48 - £58
Athens	”	1 or 2 weeks	£99
Bangkok	”	2 weeks	£385
Barcelona	”	1 or 2 weeks	£80
Berlin	”	2 to 7 days	£70
Boston	”	1 or 2 weeks	£180
Chicago	”	1 or 2 weeks	£180
Detroit	”	1 or 2 weeks	£180
Dubai	”	8 days	£190
Gaborone	”	22 days	£400
Hong Kong	”	2 or 3 weeks	£460
Jersey	”	day return	£30
Jersey	”	2 to 5 days	£45
Johannesburg	”	3 weeks	£510
Kuala Lumpur	”	2 weeks	£345
Lisbon	”	5 to 10 days	£50

181

Destination	Flights/ Week	Length of Stay	Typical Fares
Los Angeles	"	1, 2, or 3 weeks	£220
Miami	"	15 days	£200
Montreal	"	1 week	£180
Munich	"	1 week	£70
Nairobi	"	22 days	£300
Newark	"	1 or 2 weeks	£180
New York	"	1 or 2 weeks	£180
Philadelphia	"	1 or 2 weeks	£180
Seattle	"	2 weeks	£230
Singapore	"	2 or 3 weeks	£365
Sydney	"	26 or 27 days	£650
Tel Aviv	"	1 or 2 weeks	£165
Toronto	"	1 or 2 weeks	£180
Washington	"	1 week	£180

As you can see, the list of destinations is much the same as that offered by POLO; all that varies is the price.

You can book over the phone. If the flight you book is less than seven weeks away, you must pay in full immediately. Otherwise, a non-refundable deposit of £120 is due within four days, with the remainder due seven weeks before the flight date. Bookings for most destinations can be made up to four months in advance. Shades requires you to have insurance.

182

Shades is a full-service travel agency, which means they can offer "onward flights to connect with the courier flights and air passes in most countries."

They also offer discounted, non-courier fares from several cities on the West Coast of the United States to Pacific Rim destinations. The fares (£600 to Bangkok, £560 to Tokyo, for example) become more attractive the cheaper the pound. When the exchange rate is flirting with $2.00 for one pound (as it was at press time), you can almost certainly do better with a States-side consolidator. Shades also offers consolidated tickets from Toronto, Boston, New York, Washington, Miami, and Chicago to Australia (£710) and New Zealand (£620), as well as a New York to London ticket on Kuwait Air for £276 round-trip.

Speedbird Courier
British Airways World Cargo Centre
Box 99
London Heathrow Airport
Hounslow
Middlesex TW6 2JA
(081) 562-6279
(081) 562-6220 (Fax)
Speedbird services 63 destinations world-wide. It books all its on-board couriers through Courier Travel Services, Shades International Travel, and POLO Express (see above).

Speedbird Courier is a wholesale courier service created by British Airways in 1983 but operated separately. It positions itself in the marketplace as a neutral party that "purchases" British Airways tickets, locates couriers, and then allows anyone to "co-load" on their courier flights. They ship none of their own freight — that is, they don't compete with other air freight companies for retail business.

A number of air freight companies that used to find their own couriers now deal with Speedbird. If you call up a courier company and are told, "Oh, we don't need on-board couriers anymore. We have a special arrangement with the airline," they are probably dealing with Speedbird. And they're wrong, of course. They do need on-boards, it's just that Speedbird is taking care of it for them.

For the European market, Speedbird says it uses retired British Airways employees exclusively. I suspect they must, at least occassionally, have to turn to the outside when they come up short. These runs have very short turnarounds, however — a few hours at most — and would probably not be attractive to the casual courier. Of the European destinations, only Barcelona and Athens have comfortable turnarounds and these use on-board couriers, as do their other world-wide destinations. In fact, Speedbird says they service the entire world except Australia where, so they say, a recent agreement with Australian customs has obviated the need to have a passenger accompanying expedited shipments.

Sprint International Express
Unit 4, The Mercury Centre
Central Way
Feltham
Middlesex TW14 0RN
(081) 751-1111
(081) 890-9090 (Fax)
This company once booked couriers in its own right but, like many of the London courier companies, is now co-loading with Speedbird. When they have the occasional need for one of their own couriers, they find them, so I am told, within the ranks of their office staff. Still, avid couriers may want to write to Sprint, signalling their interest in serving as last-minute couriers should the need ever arise.

TNT Express Worldwide
Unit 6, Spitfire Way
Spitfire Trading Estate
Heston
Middlesex TW5 9NW
(081) 561-2345
(081) 848-3285 (Fax)
TNT flies to such U.S. destinations as Boston, New York, Philadelphia, Washington, Atlanta, Chicago, Dallas, San Francisco, Los Angeles, and Seattle. They also service Johannesburg, Nairobi, and Harare in Africa, as well as other major cities throughout the world.

They used to book freelance on-board couriers direct but now direct all enquiries to Courier Travel Services (see above). In fact, TNT is now co-loading through wholesalers which means that, since they are not buying the ticket, they can't put you on a flight. The same holds true of their own employees; free courier travel used to be a perk of employment but no longer.

Courier industry insiders tell me that TNT still needs the occasional on-board for special shipments in special circumstances. If you're available for this sort of thing and would like to play the extremely long odds, correspond with the Line Haul Manager at the above address but don't hold your breath waiting for a reply.

Trans-Africa Express
Unit 2, River Gardens Business Centre
Spur Road, North Feltham Trading Estate
Feltham
Middlesex TW14 0SN
(081) 890-4242
(081) 890-4048 (Fax)
Trans-Africa used to book freelance couriers to Nairobi and Johannesburg at round-trip fares of between £450 and £550,

depending on the time of year. At press time, Naresh Sidpia informed me that they have discontinued the service "temporarily" due to a rise in airfares but that they hope to resume service in the future. I suspect that British Airways' Speedbird Courier service (see above) has put a crimp in their operation.

World Speed Express
Unit 12, Bedfont Trading Estate
Bedfont Road
Feltham
Middlesex TW14 8EF
(081) 893-7744
(081) 893-2757 (Fax)
World Speed, in common with many other courier companies, tends to send their own staff on courier trips as a company "perk." However, they are interested in hearing from anyone who is able to travel on short notice.

They say that, since their customers often ask to send items on short notice, they cannot always find a staff member who is free to make the journey — that's where you come in. In exchange for being able to fly at the last minute, you will often be charged nothing for the trip.

World Speed reports that they have quite a few people contacting them for flights. Unfortunately, due to the world-wide recession, there have been fewer courier flights of late. "Our customers are not so much cutting down on shipments as they are switching to cheaper forms of shipment which don't require on-board couriers," explains their operations manager.

You can increase your chances of getting a free flight by volunteering to go anywhere. Simply call and leave a number where they can reach you at the last minute. Contact Miss Stubbs, the Operations Manager.

Other Overseas Contacts

T hese contacts have been gathered from various sources. Some are the foreign offices of companies listed earlier. What little information I have on them is listed. If no information is included with the entry, it is safe to assume that the company has been included solely because it identifies itself as an air courier company; it may or may not use freelancers.

ARGENTINA
Air Facility
Esmeralda 643, 4°B
Buenos Aires, Argentina
(54) (1) 3220-7720
Telex: 23185 WAYSA

I.E.S.A. Rushcourier
Avenue Pases Colon, 417
Buenos Aires, Argentina 1063
(54) (1) 301030/39

AUSTRALIA
Courier Travel Services
Sydney, New South Wales
(61) (2) 698-3753

International Courier Travel
Sydney, New South Wales
(61) (2) 317-3193

Jupiter Air Australia Pty., Ltd.
Unit 5, 154-166 O'Riordan Street
Mascot [near Sydney], New South Wales 2020
(61) (2) 317-2113
(61) (2) 317-2238 (Fax)

Qantas Cargo Terminal
Melbourne International Airport
Melbourne, Victoria 3043
(61) (018) 293-815

Qantas Cargo Terminal
Brisbane International Airport
Brisbane, Queensland 4007
(61) (018) 749-902

Qantas Cargo Terminal
Perth International Airport
Perth, Western Australia 6105
(61) (018) 916-081

BRAZIL
Air Facility
Rua Joaquin Silva 11, Conj. 706
Rio de Janeiro - RJ
(55) (021) 252-9597
Telex: 391-Z139547 JSER-BRA

CHILE
Air Facility
Huerfanos 1160, 2° OF214

Santiago de Chile
(56) (2) 698-8125
Telex: 240869 FIGUE

**2L Transportes and
Telecommunicaciones**
Estajo 360 Of. 803
Santiago de Chile
(56) (2) 394474
(56) (2) 336672 (Fax)

CHINA (HONG KONG)
Courier Travel Services
Hong Kong
(852) (03) 305-1413

International Courier Travel
Hong Kong
(852) (03) 718-1332

Jupiter Air, Ltd.
Suite 1701, 17th Floor, Tower 1
China Hong Kong City, 33 Conton Road
Tsimshatshui, Kowloon [Hong Kong]
(852) (05) 735-1886

Line Haul Express
A division of Cathay Pacific.
Hong Kong
(852) (03) 735-2167
Sophia Lai.

Wholepoint Ltd.
(852) (03) 718-0333

CHINA (TAIWAN)
Jupiter International Co., Ltd.
1/F, #23, Lane 100 Sung-Chiang Road
Taipei, Republic of China 10428
(886) (2) 551-2198

ECUADOR
Air Facility
Avenida Orellana 1791 - 6° piso
Quito, Ecuador
(593) (2) 566-233
Telex: 22806 PANAT ED

FRANCE
Jet Services Roissy
Batiment 3416
Module 700
Route du Midi
95707 Roissy
(33) (14) 862-6222
(33) (14) 862-6246 (Fax)

ISRAEL
Morseval Services, Ltd.
39 Y.L. Peretz Street
Tel Aviv, Israel 66854
(972) (3) 380-343

GERMANY
Jupiter
Flughafen-Frechtzentrum
Tor 26, Geb 451F, Room 4582
6000 Frankfort Main 75
(49) (69) 690-2833

ITALY
International Cargo Systems, Inc.
Centro Commerciale Lotto 8
Milano, San Felice 20090
Segrate, Milan

JAPAN
Jupiter Japan Co., Ltd.
Room 410 New Wall Heights
Takanawa Building B
27-7 Shirogane-Dai, 2-Chome
Minato-Ku, Tokyo 108
(81) (03) 444-6771

5/F, Compa Oobayashi Building
8-12 Hotarugaike-Nishimachi 2-Chome
Toyonaka, Osaka 560
(81) (06) 845-0521

KOREA
First Courier
First Building, 394-44, Seogy-Dong
MapoKu, Seoul 121-210
(82) (02) 324-5711
(82) (02) 754-9181

Jupiter Express Co., Ltd.
663-12 Kong Hang Dong
Kang Suh-Ku
Seoul, Republic of Korea
(82) (02) 665-6024
(82) (02) 665-1777 (Fax)

MEXICO
Mex Courier
Mexico City
(52) (5) 689-2944
(52) (5) 689-8622
Graciela Morales

NEW ZEALAND
Quickmail International
P.O. Box 53110
Auckland International Airport
Auckland
(64) (09) 275-1683

SINGAPORE
Jupiter Singapore Pte. Ltd.
Block C, Cargo Agents Building
07-04 Airport Cargo Road
Singapore 1781
(65) 545-9113

SPAIN
Prime Express
Mattias Turrion, 1-3, 2, °C
28043 Madrid
(34) (1) 200-1546
(34) (1) 759-7745

THAILAND
Siam Trans International Co. Ltd.
78 Kiatnakin Building
Bushlane, New Road
Bangkok 10500
(66) (2) 235-6741
Agent for Jupiter.

Destination Index

T his city index gives you a quick way of finding out which courier companies go where you want to go. For each destination, I have listed the names of the courier companies that fly there and the city in which those companies are located. Refer back to the appropriate listing in the "International Air Courier Directory" for more information.

Not all the destinations listed here are mentioned in the text and some destinations require making connections. An asterisk (*) indicates that the company in question either offers the destination only occasionally or that it used to fly there but doesn't at present. Some of the defunct runs may be reinstated. I suspect, however, that many are things of the past. Still, hope springs eternal, as they say, and if you are hoping for a courier flight to Auckland, this index will at least point you toward your most likely candidates.

Always remember that some destinations may not be available when you call, others may have been dropped, and others added. The courier business is the living embodiment of Toffler's dictum that "the only constant is change."

Abu Dhabi, United Arab Emirates
    POLO (London)
    Shades (England)

Amsterdam, Netherlands
    Courier Travel (NY)
    DTI (NY)
    Halbart (NY)
    Now Voyager (NY)
    POLO (London)
    Shades (England)

Asuncion, Paraguay
    Intertrade (Miami)

Athens, Greece
    Courier Travel (NY)*
    Halbart (NY)*
    Now Voyager (NY)*
    POLO (London)
    Shades (England)

Auckland, New Zealand
    ANZ (LA)*
    CTS (London)*
    POLO (London)*
    World (LA)*

Bahrain
    CTS (London)*

Bangkok, Thailand
    CTS (London)*
    DHL Int'l (London)*
    IBC (LA)

Bangkok, Thailand (cont'd)
>Jupiter (LA)*
>Jupiter (NY)*
>Jupiter (SF)*
>Now Voyager (NY)*
>POLO (LA)
>POLO (London)
>Shades (England)
>UTL (SF)

Barcelona, Spain
>POLO (London)
>Shades (England)

Basel, Switzerland
>CTS (London)*

Berlin, Germany
>POLO (London)
>Shades (England)

Bogota, Colombia
>Intertrade (Miami)
>LAC (Miami)

Boston, USA
>POLO (London)
>Shades (England)

Brussels, Belgium
>Courier Travel (NY)
>DTI (NY)
>Halbart (NY)
>Now Voyager (NY)

Buenos Aires, Argentina
      Air Facility (NY)
      Courier Travel (NY)
      DTI (NY)
      Intertrade (Miami)
      Line Haul (Miami)
      Now Voyager (NY)

Cairo, Egypt
      DHL Int'l (London)*

Caracas, Venezuela
      A-1 (Miami)
      Air Facility (NY)
      Canadex (NY)*
      Courier Travel (NY)
      DTI (NY)
      Intertrade (Miami)
      Line Haul (Miami)
      Now Voyager (NY)

Chicago, USA
      CTS (London)*
      POLO (London)
      Shades (England)

Copenhagen, Denmark
      Courier Travel (NY)
      DTI (NY)
      Halbart (NY)
      Now Voyager (NY)

Costa Rica (See San Jose, Costa Rica)

Dallas, USA
    CTS (London)

Detroit, USA
    POLO (London)
    Shades (England)

Djakarta, Indonesia
    Way To Go (LA)

Dubai, United Arab Emirates
    CTS (London)
    POLO (London)
    Shades (England)

Dublin, Ireland
    Courier Travel (NY)*
    Halbart (NY)*
    Now Voyager (NY)*
    POLO (London)*

Dusseldorf, Germany
    Halbart (NY)*

Frankfort, Germany
    Courier Travel (NY)
    DTI (NY)
    Halbart (NY)
    Now Voyager (NY)
    World (NY)*

Gaborone, Botswana
    POLO (London)
    Shades (England)

Geneva, Switzerland
    CTS (London)*
    Now Voyager (NY)

Guatemala City, Guatemala
    Line Haul (Miami)
    Trans-Air (Miami)

Guayaquil, Ecuador
    Intertrade (Miami)
    Line Haul (Miami)

Harare, Zimbabwe
    CTS (London)*

Helsinki, Finland
    Courier Travel (NY)*
    Halbart (NY)*
    Now Voyager (NY)*

Hong Kong, China
    Courier Travel (NY)
    CTS (London)
    DTI (NY)
    DHL Int'l (London)*
    F.B. (Toronto)
    IBC (LA)
    Jupiter (LA)
    Jupiter (NY)
    Jupiter (SF)
    Line Haul (London)
    Now Voyager (NY)
    POLO (LA)
    POLO (London)
    POLO (SF)

London, England
        Able (NY)
        Courier Travel (NY)
        DHL (Chicago)*
        DTI (NY)
        Excalibur (LA)*
        F.B. (Montreal)
        F.B. (Toronto)
        F.B. (Vancouver)
        Halbart (NY)
        IBC (LA)*
        IBC (NY)*
        Intermail (NY)
        Midnite (LA)
        Now Voyager (NY)
        POLO (NY) (SF) (LA)
        Priority (NY)
        TNT (Toronto)*
        TNT (SF)*
        UTL (SF)
        Way To Go (LA)*
        World (NY)*

Los Angeles, USA
        CTS (London)
        Jupiter (London)*
        Now Voyager (NY)*
        POLO (London)
        Shades (England)

Madrid, Spain
        Courier Travel (NY)
        DTI (NY)
        Halbart (Miami)
        Halbart (NY)
        Now Voyager (NY)

Montevideo, Uruguay
    Air Facility (NY)
    Courier Travel (NY)
    DTI (NY)
    Intertrade (Miami)

Montreal, Canada
    CTS (London)*
    F.B. (London)
    POLO (London)
    Shades (England)

Munich, Germany
    POLO (London)
    Shades (England)

Nairobi, Kenya
    CTS (London)
    POLO (London)
    Shades (England)
    Trans-Africa (London)*

New York, USA
    Air Action (London)*
    CTS (London)
    Jet Services (London)
    Now Courier (LA)*
    Now Voyager (NY)*
    POLO (London)
    Priority (London)*
    Shades (England)

Newark, USA
    POLO (London)
    Shades (England)

Oslo, Norway
  Courier Travel (NY)*
  DTI (NY)*
  Halbart (NY)*
  Now Voyager (NY)*

Panama City, Panama
  Intertrade (Miami)
  Line Haul (Miami)

Paris, France
  Able (NY)
  Courier Travel (NY)
  CTS (London)
  DTI (NY)
  F.B. (Montreal)
  Halbart (NY)
  Jet Services (Montreal)
  Now Voyager (NY)

Penang, Malaysia
  Way To Go (LA)

Philadelphia, USA
  POLO (London)
  Shades (England)

Pittsburgh, USA
  POLO (London)

Quito, Ecuador
  Intertrade (Miami)
  Line Haul (Miami)

Rio de Janeiro, Brazil
>Air Facility (NY)
>Courier Travel (NY)
>CTS (London)
>DHL Int'l (London)*
>DTI (NY)
>Intertrade (Miami)
>Line Haul (Miami)
>Now Voyager (NY)

Rome, Italy
>CTS (London)*
>Courier Travel (NY)
>DTI (NY)
>Halbart (NY)
>Now Voyager (NY)

San Francisco, USA
>CTS (London)

San Jose, Costa Rica
>Line Haul (Miami)
>Trans-Air (Miami)

San Juan, Puerto Rico
>Rush (NY)

Santiago, Chile
>Air Facility (NY)
>Courier Travel (NY)
>DTI (NY)
>Intertrade (Miami)
>Line Haul (Miami)
>Now Voyager (NY)
>Security (Miami)

Santo Domingo, Dominican Republic
    Line Haul (Miami)

Seattle, USA
    POLO (London)
    Shades (England)

Seoul, Korea
    East-West (NY)*
    Jupiter (LA)*
    Now Voyager (NY)*
    World (LA)

Singapore
    CTS (London)*
    IBC (LA)
    Jupiter (LA)
    Jupiter (NY)*
    Jupiter (SF)
    Now Voyager (NY)
    POLO (London)
    POLO (SF)
    Shades (England)
    UTL (SF)
    Way To Go (LA)
    Way To Go (SF)
    World (LA)*

Stockholm, Sweden
    Courier Travel (NY)
    DTI (NY)
    Halbart (NY)
    Now Voyager (NY)

Sydney, Australia
      ANZ (LA)*
      CTS (London)
      East-West (NY)*
      Excalibur (LA)*
      IBC (LA)*
      Jupiter (LA)*
      Jupiter (London)
      Now Voyager (NY)*
      POLO (London)
      Shades (England)
      Way To Go (LA)

Taipei, China
      IBC (LA)*
      Now Voyager (NY)*

Tel Aviv, Israel
      Courier Network (NY)
      Courier Travel (NY)
      Shigur/Cosell (NY)*
      POLO (London)
      Shades (England)

Tokyo, Japan
      CTS (London)
      DHL Int'l (London)*
      IBC (LA)
      Jupiter (Hong Kong)
      Now Voyager (NY)
      POLO (NY)

Toronto, Canada
      CTS (London)
      F.B. (London)

Toronto, Canada (cont'd)
    POLO (London)
    Shades (England)

Vancouver, Canada
    CTS (London)*
    Line Haul (Hong Kong)

Vienna, Austria
    CTS (London)*

Washington, D.C., USA
    POLO (London)
    Shades (England)

Zurich, Switzerland
    Courier Travel (NY)
    DTI (NY)
    Halbart (NY)
    Now Voyager (NY)
    World (NY)*

DESTINATION NOTES

Air Courier Glossary

Casual courier: A person who serves as a freelance courier from time to time. You and me!

Control the book: Very often, for any given courier run there will be one person or company who handles the details of booking couriers for that particular route. Other companies or booking agents may offer courier seats on the run but will always have to route the bookings through this person. This person is said to "control the book" for that particular courier run. It is very difficult if not impossible to determine who controls the book for any given run.

Courier pouch: Just a fancy name for the envelope containing the manifest (see below).

Co-loading: The practice of two or more courier companies sharing a single courier's baggage allotment.

Gateway: A city in which express shipments are consolidated for overseas shipment. For example, express shipments from Birmingham and Glasgow to New York would be consolidated in London, the gateway.

Line haul: Movement of air freight from one airport to another. Sometimes used to refer to the movement of freight from station to airport to airport to station.

Lock-out: The latest time at which a parcel can be accepted for courier shipment. Courier companies like to have the latest possible lock-out, so as to better serve their customers. That is why courier flights are generally the last flight of the day and why the courier tends to be the last person checked aboard the flight.

Manifest: The paperwork that accompanies a courier shipment. As a courier you will carry the manifest (usually) in a large, sealed envelope.

Pouch: An individual bag containing envelopes and parcels being shipped with an on-board courier. Today, these "pouches" are actually large, semi-transparent, heavy-duty plastic bags. Some of them resemble Army duffel bags. A single pouch can hold about 70 pounds of cargo. Sometimes, the term "courier pouch" will be applied to the sealed envelope containing the shipment manifests that the on-board courier carries on his or her person during the flight.

Retailer: A freight company that sells expedited delivery services to the general public. Federal Express, DHL, TNT, as well as hundreds of smaller companies calling themselves "air courier services" are retailers. Some retailers also ship their own expedited cargo, either on chartered planes (Federal Express) or on regularly scheduled airlines as passenger's baggage (World Courier). Others turn their expedited shipments over to wholesalers (see below).

Returning courier: A courier on a flight that is taking him or her back to the city of origin.

Rostering: The process of filling available courier seats with couriers.

Run: A round-trip between Point A and Point B.

Wholesaler: A company that specializes in handling courier shipments for other companies. A wholesaler will negotiate special tariffs with the airlines based on the volume they bring in. A wholesaler like Halbart in New York may be putting courier bags from several different courier companies on each flight it books. Some wholesalers do some retailing on the side, others (like Halbart) are 100% wholesalers.

Keep In Touch!

Now that you've read this book, I hope you'll take advantage of this last great bargain in international travel to see the world and make your travel dreams come true.

I also hope you'll keep in touch and share your air courier adventures with me so I can share them with others in future editions of *The Insiders Guide To Air Courier Bargains*.

As I've said several times in this book, the courier world is constantly changing. I'm making every effort to keep on top of these changes so I can keep you informed. But I can't be everywhere and I'll probably miss some things.

So if you find any — and I mean any — new information, let me know. If you discover a new courier company anywhere in the world, drop me a line. Or if you have a tip that can make courier travel easier or more enjoyable, I'd like to know about that, too.

I'll make sure that your information is included in the next edition of *The Insiders Guide*. I'll also acknowledge your contribution and send you a free copy.

Thanks!

> Kelly Monaghan
> Box 438
> New York, NY 10034
> (212) 304-2207

Subject Index

Note: This subject index covers, primarily, Chapters 1 through 8 of the text. The names of companies listed in the "International Air Courier Directory" are also included here. However, to locate cities to which particular courier companies offer service, consult the Destination Index.

Resources for the Intrepid Traveler
More Money-Saving Books from Inwood Training Publications

The Vacation Home Exchange And Hospitality Guide
John Kimbrough
$14.95   ©1991   ITEM # 001

Discover a new world of affordable vacation travel! Say goodbye to over-priced, inadequate hotels by swapping homes with like-minded people throughout the world. John Kimbrough gives you a complete guide to —
- Vacation home exchanges — cost-free, including car swap.
- Hospitality exchanges — free or low-cost lodging, often with meals included.
- Bed-and-breakfast exchanges — at a fraction of the usual cost.

This is the most current listing of the many exchange clubs in the U.S., Canada, England, and around the world. Learn what each club has to offer and where ... Which clubs are right for you ... Each club's strengths and weaknesses ... How to find the exchange you want ... The easy way to go about making an exchange.

> "Go for it! We have stayed in a 300-year-old fieldstone cottage in the Cotswolds, a remodelled manor house in Essex, an ultra-modern apartment in Bonn, and a comfortable chalet in Switzerland."
> D. B.
> Sacramento, CA

The Insider's Guide To Cruise Discounts
Cpt. Bill Miller
$12.95   ©1991   ITEM # 002

ATTENTION! Couples, single travelers, honeymooners, wheelchair travelers, jetsetters: If you want to cruise aboard the best ships and pay the lowest price — YOU NEED THIS BOOK! Learn all the secrets you need to ... Cruise on the best ships at the lowest prices ... Get celebrity treatment on your next cruise ... Buy travel at below wholesale prices ... Qualify for deep, deep, last-minute discounts ... Convince a reluctant spouse to take a cruise ... Cruise free!

WARNING! Failure to purchase this book could mean you'll overpay hundreds of dollars for your next cruise!

How To Get A Job With A Cruise Line
Mary Fallon Miller
$12.95   ©1992   **ITEM # 003**
WANTED! Adults of all ages, backgrounds, skills, and talents. To fill broad range of positions in the booming cruise line industry. Successful applicants will enjoy adventure, travel, romance, and a steady paycheck.
If you have ever dreamed of running away to work on the Love Boat, you need this book. Mary Miller gives you the Insider's Advantage to getting hired. It's like having a relative in the cruise line business.
How To Get A Job With A Cruise Line tells you precisely to whom, how, when, and where to apply. This book will save you hundreds of dollars, hours of wasted time, and endless frustration. Filled with insider's tips from successful people who are living their dream of working on cruise ships, including:
- How do I get hired by a cruise line?
- How can I use my current skills?
- What are the different jobs like?
- What exciting places can I travel to?

If you want to work on the Love Boat (and who doesn't?) this book will give you the winning edge you need to beat the competition for these dream jobs!
"Thanks! It's about time someone took the trouble to get the correct information to the public."
Cheryl B. Clahr
Director of Personnel, American Hawaii Cruises
Endorsed by Cruise Line International Association (CLIA)

Plan 'n' Pack
Susanne Reyto
$21.95   ©1991   **ITEM # 004**
Travel light, smart, organized with this "state-of-the art" video guide. Plan 'n' Pack presents a lifetime of travel secrets from an industry expert. Susanne Reyto, noted travel expert, shares her knowledge and experience with you in this informative video guide to planning, packing, safety, and security made easy. Filled with tips and practical suggestions that have helped many business and leisure travelers eliminate their anxieties and increase their travel pleasure. Included are suggestions for what to take ... how to select a color scheme ... creating a well-organized travel wardrobe ... choice of luggage ... how to pack wrinkle-free ... safety and security abroad ... and much, much more. **VHS only!**
"State-of-the-art!"
Travel Agent magazine
Endorsed by American Society of Travel Agents (ASTA)

How To Get Paid $30,000 A Year To Travel (Without Selling Anything)
Craig Chilton
$24.95   ©1991   **ITEM # 005**

Have you ever seen a Winnebago transported on the back of a truck? Or an ambulance? A hearse? A fire truck? Or a UPS truck? Chances are you never have.

Craig Chilton, author of HOW TO GET PAID $30,000 A YEAR TO TRAVEL *(Without Selling Anything)*, will tell you why the delivery of recreational and specialty vehicles is America's greatest "sleeper" travel lifestyle. There are about 50,000 people throughout the USA and Canada who do this all the time, on a full-time or part-time basis, working for more than 1,000 manufacturers and transporter companies.

Here are some basic facts:
*   In all states and provinces, all you need is an ordinary driver's license to deliver RVs. (Larger specialty vehicles require a chauffeur's license.)
*   All companies provide full insurance coverage for vehicles and their drivers.
*   All vehicles are new, so they're covered by manufacturer's warranty in case of breakdown.
*   Companies pay all road expenses and return transportation, apart from earnings. (Earnings normally are based on the number of miles driven per trip.) Drivers who fly home normally get to keep all their Frequent Flyer miles.
*   This lifestyle is nothing like trucking. No freight. Very few regulations. It's like getting paid to drive one's own car.
*   College students (18 and over) are needed during the summer months to supplement the regular work force. They typically earn $8,000-$12,000 during that season.
*   30 percent are retired people over age 65 who never worry about a "fixed income." (There's no upper age limit. As long as a person is a safe driver, he's in demand, due to his experience and maturity.)

Craig Chilton has appeared on more than 500 talk shows to inform the public about this profitable and fun lifestyle.This **NEW, 1991-1992 EDITION** reveals Craig's system for maximizing this exciting lifestyle and lists more than 3,000 potential employers throughout the US, Canada, Europe, and Australia!

Who hasn't dreamed of getting paid to travel?
Now you can find out how.

A COMPLETE CAREER SYSTEM FOR JUST $24.95

The Insiders Guide To Air Courier Bargains — How To Travel World-Wide For Next To Nothing
Kelly Monaghan
$14.95   ©1992   **ITEM # 006**

Paris for $199! Mexico City for $99! Hong Kong for free! Sound impossible? It's not!

Every day, hundreds of people take off for exotic ports of call as air couriers. Those sitting next to them on the plane have no idea of their "secret mission." They certainly don't know that the courier beside them paid only a fraction of the lowest available fare. In fact, the courier might even be flying **for free!** An air courier is someone who accompanies time-sensitive cargo shipped as passengers' luggage on regularly scheduled airlines. Sometimes these people are employees of air freight companies. Most of the time they are "freelancers," ordinary people — like you! — who perform a valuable service for the air freight company in exchange for a deep, deep discount on their round-trip air fare.

Being an air courier requires no training, no advanced degrees, no special knowledge of the air freight business. **Anyone can be an air courier.** All it takes is a yen for low-cost travel, a taste for adventure, and the right insider contacts — contacts that *The Insiders Guide To Air Courier Bargains* provides in abundance.

Here's what people have been saying about *The Insiders Guide To Air Courier Bargains* —

"Everything you need to know."
Travel & Leisure
"A comprehensive overview."
Consumer Reports Travel Letter
"If you've ever dreamed of seeing the world but thought you could never afford to do it, this is the book for you!"
Worldwide Investment News
"I really appreciate your book and the specific names and numbers you present. It is something that can be put to practical use, instantly. And what's fantastic is, it works!"
D. A. F.
Willoughby Hills, OH
"Had it not been for your book, I would never have known about getting on the list for further discounts or free travel. Thanks!"
F. P.
Concord, CA

Consolidators: Air Travel's Bargain Basement
Kelly Monaghan
$4.00   © 1991   ITEM # 007
In this Special Report, Kelly Monaghan unlocks the secrets of the world of "consolidators" — travel specialists who buy huge blocks of seats from the airlines at deep discounts and then pass those savings on to you. Lists scores of consolidators across the U.S., both those who deal directly with the public and those you can work with through your travel agent. Learn how to ...
- Get "super-saver" fares, even when the deadline has passed!
- Get an additional 5% off any flight you book yourself!
- Book by phone and receive your tickets in the mail!

This Special Report is yours FREE when you order any other book! (If ordered separately, there is no postage and handling charge.)

Free America! A State-By-State Guide To Things To See And Do Absolutely Free
Kelly Monaghan
$9.95 each volume   © 1992
There may be no such thing as a free lunch and there is certainly no such thing as a cholesterol-free lunch but there are still thousands of things to see and do in these United States that won't cost you one red cent. That's the inevitable conclusion after browsing through the four volumes of *Free America!*, an exhaustive state-by-state directory of some of America's hidden treasures. From the sublime (Toad Suck Park, Arkansas) to the ridiculous (the New York Stock Exchange), *Free America!* gives you the low-down on thousands of attractions that, in this day of ever-increasing prices, are still free for the knowledgeable traveler to see and experience. In four volumes:

Vol. 1: The Northeast   ITEM # 008
(Maine, New Hampshire, Vermont, Massachusetts, Rhode Island, Connecticut, New York, New Jersey, Pennsylvania, Delaware, Maryland, West Virginia)

Vol. 2: The South   ITEM # 009
(DC, Virginia, Kentucky, Tennessee, North Carolina, South Carolina, Mississippi, Alabama, Georgia, Florida, Arkansas, Louisiana)

Vol. 3: The Midwest   ITEM # 010
(Ohio, Michigan, Indiana, Illinois, Wisconsin, Missouri, Kansas, Iowa, Nebraska, North Dakota, South Dakota, Minnesota)

Vol. 4: The West   ITEM # 011
(Texas, Oklahoma, New Mexico, Colorado, Wyoming, Montana, Idaho, Utah, Arizona, Nevada, California, Oregon, Washington, Alaska, Hawaii)

SPECIAL OFFER! ALL FOUR VOLUMES OF *FREE AMERICA!* FOR JUST $29 (A SAVINGS OF OVER 25%)! ITEM # 012

ORDER FORM

Quantity	Item # (or title)	Price

FREE WITH YOUR ORDER!	Merchandise total	
Consolidators: Air Travel's	NY residents add 8.25% tax	
Bargain Basement	Regular postage	
($4.00 if ordered separately)	UPS Delivery	
	TOTAL (US funds only)	

Delivery Options: For regular postage (Special 4th Class Book Rate), add $3.00 for the 1st book and $.50 for each additional book ordered. Allow 3 to 4 weeks for delivery. For faster UPS delivery, add $4.00 for the 1st book and $1.00 for each additional book ordered. UPS can deliver only to street addresses (no P.O. boxes) in the continental US. For foreign delivery, compute the regular postage, then add 10% of the "merchandise total." In England, contact A.S.A.P. Publications, Prospect House, Downley Common, High Wycombe, Bucks. HP13 5XQ for prices and availability.

Name: _____

Address: _____

City: _____ State: _____ Zip: _____

Phone: _____

Make checks payable to:
Inwood Training Publications • Box 438 • New York, NY 10034-0438